Bristol City Memories

The subs bench interviews

DEDICATION

This book is dedicated to the memory of my friend Buster Footman and
to Benjamin Pritchard, who loved Bristol City and had his life cut short by a brain
tumour at just eight years old.

BRISTOL CITY MEMORIES
THE SUBS BENCH INTERVIEWS

RICHARD LATHAM

FOREWORD BY DOUG HARMAN

DESIGN AND ORIGINATION BY STEVE HENDERSON

First published in 2020 by Redcliffe Press Ltd
81g Pembroke Road, Bristol BS8 3EA

e: info@redcliffepress.co.uk
www.redcliffepress.co.uk
Follow us on:
Twitter @RedcliffePress
Facebook @RedcliffePress

ISBN 978-1-911408-76-5

British Library Cataloguing-in-Publication Data
A catalogue record for this book is available from the British Library

Redcliffe Press Ltd is committed to being an environmentally friendly publisher.
This book is made from Forest Stewardship Council® certified paper.

Design and origination by Steve Henderson
Printed and bound in the Czech Republic via Akcent Media

Contents

ACKNOWLEDGEMENTS

While many of the photographs in this book are from my own personal collection or those of the interviewees, I am indebted to the *Bristol Post, Western Daily Press,* Bristol City Media Department and Joe Meredith Productions for permission to use cuttings and pictures.

I am grateful to my co-presenter and the producer of Subs Bench, Nigel Turner, for his help and encouragement. The programme was his project from the outset, and we have both derived enormous pleasure from working on it. Thanks are also due to Doug Harman for kindly agreeing to write the foreword.

My wife Martine acted as a diligent proof-reader and I knew from my previous book, *Wembley Wonders,* that I had a very capable and experienced designer in Steve Henderson, once media manager at Ashton Gate.

Finally, to all the members of the Bristol City family who gave freely of their time to appear on Subs Bench and share their memories, I extend my sincere thanks. I hope the book does justice to their colourful stories and contributions to the club.

FOREWORD

Football is all about passion for your team, the travelling, pre-match rituals, highs and lows as games unravel over 90 minutes – moments etched in memories forever.

As a young boy growing up in London, there was no shortage of teams to follow. My grandfather and father were from north London and were ardent Tottenham Hotspur fans so it was inevitable the double-winning Spurs team of the 1960s would also become my team.

I had a good bank job, working in London, but four hours commuting each day from my home in Kent was no fun and you can imagine how I felt when the bank announced that we would be relocating to Bristol. So it was that my family moved to Portishead in 1973, with a new football team to find and support. The journey along the M4 and into Bristol via the M32 took us past Eastville and I immediately felt the Rovers were not for me. Ashton Gate, on the other hand, felt special. I was hooked from my very first City game and just in time to support the team to promotion and Division One. These were great times to be a City fan, with lots of fond memories, but tougher times were around the corner and about to get much worse!

Fortunately, things slowly improved, both on and off the pitch. By now, I had 'retired' to look after my old mum, who was suffering with Alzheimer's. Naively, I had bitten off more than I could chew and after two years she was moved into a nursing home. Lost for what to do next, I wrote to then City chairman Steve Lansdown in the hope that my skills and experience might be of some help to the club. Steve arranged for me to meet Colin Sexstone and in 2005 I started work at BCFC alongside Colin, eventually becoming chief executive, uniquely on two occasions, in 2013 and again in 2015.

I have so many fond memories of working at Ashton Gate, of cup runs, promotion seasons and trips to Wembley. However, my most treasured City memories are the times

I spent with grandson Ben, a mad keen City fan of course, who was diagnosed with an incurable and inoperable brain tumour in 2017 and died six months later, aged just eight. Ben was laid to rest in his full City home kit and I shall be forever grateful to so many good people at Ashton Gate, owners, directors, players, staff and fans for their support and kindness shown to us during such difficult days for our family. Bristol City truly is in the heart and soul of the community.

I have known Richard Latham for many years and he has spent his entire working life at the forefront of sports reporting, covering the club's highs and lows since 1979. It makes him ideally placed to pull together this extraordinary collection of memories, which I'm sure anyone with a connection to Bristol City FC will enjoy and treasure.

Doug Harman
Executive Director,
Bristol City Football Club

INTRODUCTION

When *Made in Bristol TV* wanted to launch a sports programme back in 2014, they approached Nigel Turner, an experienced broadcaster and journalist, who had worked extensively for HTV and as sports producer at *BBC Radio Bristol* since settling in the West country in the early 1980s. It was Nigel who came up with the title Subs Bench and the design of the programme, which originally featured a panel of pundits, myself among them, to discuss local sporting issues, along with film gathered during the preceding week, including press conferences at the two Bristol football clubs and Bristol Rugby.

Before long, a format developed with Nigel, who produced the programme, and I acting as co-presenters. Part of the show was devoted to nostalgia through a guest spot, filled each week largely by past City and Rovers players, but also featuring famous names from rugby, cricket and boxing, such as rugby World Cup final referee Ed Morrison, England cricketer Jack Russell and world bantamweight champion Lee Haskins.

As the only television programme of its kind in the region, Subs Bench soon gained a loyal following after first being aired in October 2014. The hour-long show was broadcast at 7pm on Friday evenings on Sky channel 117, Freeview 7 and Virgin Media 159, with repeats at 12 noon and 10pm on Tuesdays. An accompanying programme, Subs Bench Extra, was screened for half an hour on Monday evenings. By April 2016, weekly viewing figures had reached 70,000 and it was rare for Nigel and I to visit Ashton Gate or the Memorial Stadium without football or rugby fans expressing their delight over seeing local sport being given such extensive television coverage.

The first year Subs Bench was on the air coincided with one of the most memorable seasons in Bristol football history, City doing the double of League One title and Johnstone's Paint Trophy winners, while Rovers regained Football League status by beating Grimsby Town on penalties in the Conference Play-off final. Both clubs embraced the programme and we were able to highlight their successes with weekly exclusive interviews with managers and players. We followed them to Wembley and broadcast some unforgettable scenes.

The success of Lee Haskins allowed Subs Bench to go international, Nigel flying to Las Vegas for the proposed world title fight with Randy Caballero and reporting into the programme on the build-up to the event. He found himself with a major scoop when on the spot to break news of Caballero failing to make the weight and Lee being crowned champion without throwing a punch.

Another real pleasure of working on Subs Bench was covering local grassroots sport, including football and rugby cup finals. We also ensured a vast array of sports were catered for, featuring the likes of hockey, athletics, amateur boxing, bowls, fencing, American football, netball, darts and even ultimate frisbee. Matches played by Bristol City's women's team were a regular part of the show.

But most enjoyable of all for me personally was the opportunity to delve into the past with former City players, many of whom I had watched as a fan long before starting my career as a sports journalist with the *Bristol Evening Post* in 1979. To hear them recount from first-hand experience tales of some of the greatest days – and some of the saddest – in the Robins' history was always fascinating. There were plenty of surprises and no shortage of humour as we revisited past glories.

It came as a shock to Nigel and I when, in June 2017, *Made in Bristol TV* took the decision to axe Subs Bench and introduce a sports phone-in programme with a new presenter. Despite appeals on our behalf from all the major local professional clubs and many sports fans in the area, the company made it clear the decision was final. Suffice to say, the replacement format lasted a matter of weeks and soon the region was without a TV sports show again, as it has been ever since. We kept our programme going on social media and were then approached by the *Bristol Post* to do guest interviews under the Subs Bench banner for their website. This we were delighted to do and many new ones were carried out, some featured in this book, which can still be found on 'Bristol Live'. The Covid-19 pandemic brought what we hope will prove a temporary interruption to this service. But even during lockdown, we produced a new 13-part series on Facebook and YouTube, which proved equally popular.

The original Subs Bench was important to me because I had never before presented a television programme. I had often appeared as a pundit on HTV's Soccer Night with my friend Jed Pitman, but this was a chance to learn new skills, which doesn't often arise 35

FURY AS SPORT TV SHOW AXED

Made in Bristol TV *Subs Bench* presenters Nigel Turner, (right), and the Indy's Richard Latham who have covered a range of sports and welcomed a host of sportsmen and women to their studios, including Lee Haskins, Bristol's former IBF bantamweight world champion.

SUBS BENCH, the West Country's only dedicated television sports show which has been part of the Made In Bristol schedules since October 2014, has been axed – despite the company being inundated with calls for it to be retained.

The programme was hosted by local journalist Nigel Turner and the *Indy's* football and cricket correspondent Richard Latham, who each have

by John Harding

the future of local sports coverage across the West Country.

'*Subs Bench* was the only means available for sports fans to enjoy the comprehensive coverage on the television of both professional and grass-roots sports clubs who will be left with no television coverage once again.

'In two and a half years the programme has built an extremely loyal and appreciative follow-

Made in Bristol or send messages via social media expressing their dismay at the decision.'

Made in Bristol is part of the Made Television Network, which claims to be the largest operator of city TV stations in the UK with channels having a weekly reach well over one million viewers.

Made TV chief executive James Conway said: 'We always allow editorial decisions to be made at a local level rather than at a corporate level.

'While I appreciate viewers' frustrations when programming changes are made, I can assure you that these decisions are not taken lightly and

years into a career. Nigel proved a patient teacher and after initial nerves I came to love the show. We met so many great people, involved not just in West country sport, but from the international stage, such as former world heavyweight champion Larry Holmes and England rugby's Vunipola brothers.

Above all, Subs Bench was fun. We even had a singing contribution during the Made in Bristol days when Gerry Francis appeared on the programme and brought along his son Adam, looking to make a name in the world of rock music. Nigel took on Raymond van Barneveld at darts and tried his hand at bowls, with equal lack of success! There was also the day when former Bristol City boss Gary Johnson came into the studio on a Sunday and was just about to head off for his roast lunch when it was discovered the sound hadn't been recorded. We had to do the whole half-hour programme again after Gary made a quick phone call home, telling his wife to keep the meat in the oven!

Hopefully, this book conveys the enjoyment we derived from talking football with so many fascinating interviewees. Whether Nigel and I are involved or not, I sincerely hope the West country does have a TV sports show again in the future. Subs Bench proved how much supporters and players at all levels want to see their clubs featured on screen and given in-depth coverage lasting more than a matter of seconds as an insert into news programmes.

The interviews that follow were conducted between 2014 and 2020, the eras covered going back as far as the 1960s when I first started attending City games. Every player featured I watched, either from the old Grand Stand, as a supporter, or from the press box. Readers may notice feint autographs on some of the photos, which I purchased and got signed when the club won promotion to the old First Division in 1976, three years before I began my career as a journalist. The scarf pictured on the back cover is another souvenir from those days.

Professional football careers are relatively short, in some cases tragically so because of injury, which makes it all the more important for players to store memories of their best days. The same applies to directors, staff and supporters, because they also experience the roller-coaster of emotions that go with following a club like Bristol City, whose colourful history is liberally sprinkled with highs and lows.

This book has been a genuine labour of love. It seems only yesterday that I was being thrilled by goals from John Galley and Chris Garland, leading the attack for a team playing in an all-red strip. Leaping out of my seat to acclaim Clive Whitehead's winning goal against Portsmouth on that unforgettable night of April 20th 1976. Or watching proudly in the Highbury sunshine as City outplayed Arsenal a few months later and Paul Cheesley's header announced the club's return to the top flight of English football after an absence of 65 years.

Readers of all ages will have their own special memories and hopefully this book will rekindle some that have faded. Let's all wallow in some unbridled sporting nostalgia.

Richard Latham

LOUIS CAREY

1995-2004 & 2005-2014

A product of the School of Excellence, which preceded City's Academy, Louis Carey made his first team debut at York City in October 1995 and went on to make 646 appearances, beating the club record previously held by John Atyeo. Apart from a short spell with Coventry City, he spent his entire career at Ashton Gate, representing the Robins at both the old and new Wembley stadiums and being part of two promotion squads, while also helping to lift the LDV Vans Trophy in 2003.

What games out of the 646 you played for City stand out in your memory?

I particularly enjoyed the two matches against Watford when we were vying with them to win what was then the Second Division championship during the 1997-98 season. It was my first promotion campaign after only a couple of years in the team and I found it so exciting. When you are a young player you think every season is going to bring success and I remember the older lads telling me to savour every

moment because it wouldn't happen very often.

The games against Watford ended in 1-1 draws and I felt I played well in both. Playing at the old Wembley and the new one were fantastic experiences, as was winning the LDV Vans Trophy at Cardiff, while local derbies were always special. But if I had to pick one game for pure excitement it would be the second leg of the Second Division Play-off semi-finals against Hartlepool in May 2004. We were losing on aggregate and grabbed two late goals to turn the tie around. When Christian Roberts scored the winner, I could feel the ground shaking.

The energy around the place that night was unbelievable and it was the greatest atmosphere I played in. Most special of all was probably leading the team out at the new Wembley for the Championship Play-off final against Hull City in 2008 in front of more than 80,000 spectators. That's what dreams are made of for someone who supported the club as a kid. Unfortunately, things didn't work out for us on the day and we lost to a Dean Windass wonder goal, which left everyone gutted. But thinking back now it was still a very proud day for me.

Your appearance at the old Wembley in the 1999-2000 Auto Windscreen Shield final also ended in a narrow defeat by Stoke City. What do you recall of that day?

Leroy Rosenior was one of a group of caretaker-managers at the time and we had a lot of young players because there was not a lot of money to spend at the club. That meant there was an incredible feeling of excitement about playing at Wembley against what was a very strong Stoke side. Unfortunately, memories of the game are clouded for me because my mistake led to the winning goal. They were awarded a free kick from outside the box and I stepped forward a few yards to remonstrate with the referee because I didn't think it was a foul. I went past the ball and Stoke took the kick quickly, which meant I was out of position when they crossed and scored. It was a great opportunity for us to turn over a big club with a huge following and I learned an important lesson the hard way. Since becoming a coach, I have told young players about what happened and used it as an example of the need to stay switched on at all times.

Let's talk about a winning appearance in a final. In April 2003 you were part of the City team who lifted the LDV Vans Trophy with a 2-0 win over Carlisle United at the Millennium Stadium.

It had been 17 years since the club had won a cup competition and, although I was not at the 1986 Freight Rover Trophy final, I had a photo up in my loft of the players on the pitch celebrating after the win over Bolton. The long wait for a City team to emulate them increased the sense of anticipation going to Cardiff. It may not have been Wembley, but it was still an incredible stadium and to take 40,000 fans across the Severn Bridge made for an unforgettable day. There was a lot of pressure on us because Carlisle were from a division below and we certainly didn't produce our best football. The pitch wasn't great, possibly because of the rugby played there, and it didn't suit our style of play. Going in at

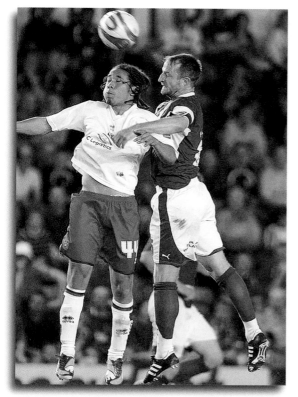

half time level increased the tension a bit, but once Lee Peacock got the first goal we relaxed and the result was never in doubt. I remember the goals and the celebrations more than the 90 minutes because in all honesty it was a poor game.

We had enjoyed a really good season leading up to it, scoring a lot of goals, but didn't fire as a team on the afternoon. Danny Wilson had built a team with a lot of young players and I felt something really special was happening at the club. One of the youngsters, Liam Rosenior, scored the second goal and went on to play at top level before becoming a TV pundit and coach. I always had a lot of time for Liam and he is excellent expressing his views on television. He has gained a lot of knowledge and experience over the course of his career and I am sure he will use it to good effect whichever path he chooses to take. I don't care what level of football you play at, winning a trophy is special, and that was certainly the case for us in Cardiff. After I finished as a professional and played for my pub team, I still found cup football a buzz.

When you add the chance to play at a magnificent stadium, it is a dream come true for all of us who grew up watching FA Cup finals on television. There is a sense of having achieved something in your career and to help make the day for so many fans produces an unbelievable feeling of satisfaction.

Ian Holloway told us in a Subs Bench interview that he felt his Bristol accent held him back and prevented him getting more job opportunities. Have you found that coming from what many regard as a backwater of football has hindered your career?

I can understand Ian's point of view. It's not that West country football isn't rated, but it is true that the way the Bristol accent has been treated by the media over the years has led to a lot of mocking. We're all seen as farmers and not viewed as intellectually clever. What Ian has proved is that his knowledge of the game, allied to his passion and drive, can overcome any stereotyping. When you are successful as a manager and take teams into the Premier League, no one cares about your accent.

Was one of the reasons you left Ashton Gate to join Coventry City that you wanted to sample life outside the West country?

No, it was more to do with circumstances at Bristol City at the time. We had just lost the

Play-off final to Brighton in 2004, Danny Wilson had been sacked and a lot of the players were being asked to take wage cuts. I think nine of us ended up leaving that summer, even though several did not want to go. I don't regret moving to Coventry because it was an amazing place, with lovely people, and it gave me the chance to play Championship football. I played under two good managers, who had worked at the highest level, and with a lot of top players.

The learning curve for me was steep, but I enjoyed that and I was in the team for 27 games. It was just in the back of my mind all the time that my burning desire was really to see my local club playing at the same level and even in the Premier League. It is an ambition I still have, whether I am part of it or not. I guess I got a bit homesick. If I hadn't joined Coventry, I might even have approached 700 games for City, but I still look back on it as a valuable, if at times tough, period in my life.

Is it a regret that you never played in the Premier League?

I don't look back and beat myself up over it. But it is probably something I should have pushed for more. Playing for your local club and having your friends and family around you can sometimes be too comfortable, but the fact was that I wanted to reach the Premier League with Bristol City. Steven Gerrard always said he wanted to win the title with Liverpool, rather than with any other club, and I felt the same about my team. I wanted to emulate the side of 1975-76 and, with the size of the city and the finances the club had at certain times, I felt it was an achievable objective. There were stages when we were on a roll and I could really see it happening, but it wasn't to be. When I reflect now, one of my strengths was reading the game and if you can do that there is every chance that you are capable of playing at top level.

Who was the best City manager you played under?

I always answer that question with a top three because I am not able to put them in any particular order. John Ward, Danny Wilson and Gary Johnson had different personalities, but each had fantastic attributes as managers and I like to think I learned from them all.

On many occasions during your playing career you made it clear you were not interested in becoming a manager yourself. As we speak, you are Southampton Under-16 coach. Have you changed your mind about the future?

Even coaching didn't hugely appeal to me while I was a player. I never knew quite why. When I look back now, I think it was because I wanted to focus totally on playing without any distractions. I also didn't like some of the egos in the game and the materialistic side of it. When I finished playing, I had a year out, doing a lot of charity work. Then I met representatives from Southampton, who made me understand what their club was all about at the time. It was about bringing young players through and that struck a chord with me. I got involved as a coach and now it is something I really want to pursue. I am in no rush to be a manager, but it's not something I would rule out.

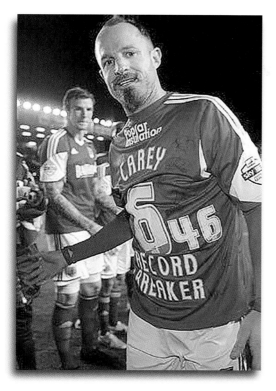

Your time as a player at Ashton Gate finally came to an end in the summer of 2014 when City decided to release you. Did you agree with that decision?

When you get to the age of 37 as a player, your body starts talking to you and telling you things you don't want to hear. Some choose to ignore it and carry on to earn a few more quid. It can lead to letting people down and I was very aware of not allowing that to happen. I never wanted to go onto the pitch feeling that I was unable to give 100 per cent for the team. I played for the Under-21s as an over-age player a lot during my last season and I knew that would be my role from the time Sean O'Driscoll was manager and he kept me on. I was alright playing the odd first team game as back-up, but I could no longer maintain form and fitness over a longer period. So the timing of my departure was right for all concerned.

To play 646 games requires an incredibly high level of fitness over a lot of years. And we are talking about a player, who once missed the start of the season through dropping a barbeque on his foot!

Thanks for bringing that up. It was a World Cup year and City had just appointed a new manager in Steve Coppell, whose arrival had created huge expectations for the season ahead. Four days before we were back for pre-season training England played Germany and I organised a get-together at home. I was dragging the barbeque along with all the food on it when I dropped it on the back of my heel. The gash went right through to the bone and I couldn't put my football boots on for a while. I still tried to play in a kick-around bare-foot that afternoon, not realising how serious the damage was. I cleaned the cut in the evening, but when I went for a run the following day, I could feel my achilles tendon moving about. I rang the physio to say I had a bit of a problem and when she saw the damage, she just put her head in her hands. There was no sense in trying to make something up, so I went in and told the new gaffer exactly what happened, promising to get myself fit again as soon as possible. It turned out that I had to cut the back out of boots to begin training again and I missed the start of the season.

You also suffered what might potentially have proved a fatal head injury in a match against Scunthorpe United at Ashton Gate. How on earth did you come back from that and start heading a ball again?

It was a clash of heads and I didn't realise at the time that I had fractured my skull. Later I was told that if the crack had gone across the bone, rather than down, there was a chance

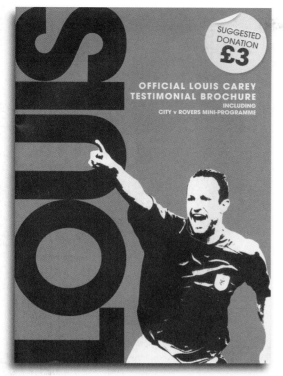

I would not have survived. I actually went on and played the second half and if I had been caught again in a similar place again it could have proved fatal. I broke my nose several times in my career and every time it happened, I couldn't wait to head a ball again to prove to myself I was okay. It was the same with the fractured skull. It's like falling off a bike or a horse. You need to get back on again as soon as possible if you are not to let it affect you. Ever since I have had trouble with my hearing, not in conversation, but in concentrating on one sound if several are being made at the same time.

There is a statue of John Atyeo at Ashton Gate, but not one of the player who beat his appearances record for City? Should there be one of you?

Perhaps if I came back as manager one day and did well. I regard it as an incredible achievement to have played 646 games for the club, but when you look at John Atyeo's career, he also played and scored for England and netted an amazing number of goals for City. It took 40 years for the club to build a statue of the great man, so maybe my time will come. But he is far more worthy of one than me. Some clubs are quicker than others to recognise the good things people have done for them over the years and I think it should be highlighted more.

PAUL CHEESLEY

Although Bristol-born, Paul Cheesley began his career at Norwich City before moving back home to sign at Ashton Gate for £30,000 in December 1973. He scored 16 goals in the promotion season of 1975-76 and the winner in the opening game of the following campaign at Arsenal before a serious knee injury, sustained against Stoke City in the next match, effectively ended his hugely promising career.

Why was it that you had to play for Norwich City before either of the Bristol clubs took note of your talent?

It was a bit odd because when I set my heart on becoming a professional footballer I wrote to both City and Rovers asking for trials. Both accepted and wanted to sign me on schoolboy forms, but there was nothing concrete and I decided to leave it, thinking that something better would come along.

It then looked as though I would leave school and get a job. I started playing for St George Easton-in-Gordano, initially in the youth team. While there I was watched by Ron Veale, who scouted in the Bristol area for Norwich City manager Ron Saunders. He arranged for me to have a trial at Carrow Road and the story began there for me. I scored my first League goal for Norwich against Liverpool and was happy at the club. But Ron Saunders left to be replaced by John Bond and by the time Alan Dicks showed interest in signing me for City I had been in the reserves for a while. I wanted first team football, so I decided to make the move back to Bristol.

Quite soon you were part of a developing City team on course for the old First Division and your strike partnership with Tom Ritchie played a big part in that.

Yes, that came about pretty much by accident. We were playing Cardiff City in a pre-season match and I was out of favour at the time, having had one or two disagreements with manager Alan Dicks. I was on the bench for the game and Keith Fear picked up an injury. Even then, the boss put Shaun Penny on ahead of me, but he was soon getting kicked to death by Cardiff's big centre-half and I was eventually introduced to sort things

EVENING POST
BRISTOL CITY
★ PROMOTION SPECIAL

"Say Cheese . . ." and here's the result, a section of the promotion-happy fans.

DIVISION ONE HERE WE COME

out. We won 1-0 and, with Keith injured, the manager asked Tom if he fancied a go up alongside me as a strike-force. That's what happened and it worked out pretty well.

We worked on the partnership over the rest of pre-season training and the rest, as they say, is history. I didn't score for the first four games of the season and then got off the mark in a derby match against Bristol Rovers. That got me going on a great run in which I scored something like 11 goals in nine games before I had a bit of hamstring trouble and my form dipped. That was when 'TV Tom' came to the fore. We called him that because he had a habit of scoring whenever we were on 'Match of the Day'. He had a great second half to the season, so between us we did the business. We were lucky to be involved in a team that had a bit of everything.

Is it fair to say that the partnership worked because you complemented each other so well, with your aerial ability and Tom's running off the ball?
I tried to model my work-rate on Tom's because I knew that if I could work as hard as he did, with what I had to offer in other respects, I would become a decent player. Tom did a lot of my running for me and a lot of the running for other members of the side. He had a massive engine, but was also a skilful player and, don't forget, he was good in the air as well.

Tell us your memories of the other players in that 1975-76 promotion team, starting with goalkeeper Ray Cashley.
Yes, 'Mad Ray'! He would probably agree with me that he was not the most technically gifted keeper in League football, compared to the likes of Peter Bonetti or Peter Shilton, but he was so brave. When it came to courage and determination, we wouldn't have swapped him for anyone. People tend to forget what a small squad we had, with only 16-

18 players, so the team was the same week-in, week-out. We had Gerry Sweeney, Gary Collier, Geoff Merrick and Brian Drysdale at the back, with Donnie Gillies able to play at right-back if Gerry moved into midfield, and David Rodgers as cover for the two centre-backs. Donnie was so quick that if he missed a tackle on the halfway line he could get back and make another one, while big Dave was very much part of a squad that was one big happy family. In midfield we had Gerry Gow. Need you say any more. He wasn't the biggest of guys, but he was massive in stature on the pitch and so brave as well.

For opponents, he was like an annoying gnat buzzing all around them, which they wanted to swat, but couldn't. He was a talented footballer too. Trevor Tainton was the rock of the team, never a ten-out-of-ten performer, but seven and a half or better every game. He would ensure stability in midfield and be the anchor when Jimmy Mann would go on his mazy dribbles. Jimmy was brilliant at using his body to stop opponents getting near him and his shooting power was fantastic. I could never understand why Leeds United let him go or how Alan Dicks found him.

Clive Whitehead broke into the team on a regular basis during the promotion season and was young, raw and exuberant. Sometimes you would think 'for goodness sake Clive what are you doing', but he grew into the side and was massively important to me with those cheeky little crosses he would play into the box.

It all culminated in the penultimate match of the season against Portsmouth at Ashton Gate, when victory would clinch promotion, and you played a part in the winning goal. What are your memories of that night?
I got a bit of a lucky flick-on when Brian Drysdale knocked a ball into the box and Clive

Nice suit and what about the kipper tie! Paul is dressed to kill for the open top bus tour of Bristol that followed promotion to the First Division

Whitehead got on the end of it to smash a fantastic half-volley into the top corner. But that was early on and we went on to have a really bad case of the jitters that night. We knew we were so close to achieving our aim and very nearly didn't make it, but we clung on and that was all that mattered. I remember that just before blowing the final whistle the referee got himself as near to the tunnel as possible because there was obviously going to be a pitch inva-sion. I wasn't as prepared and was right across the other side of the field near the Dolman Stand when the game ended. By the time I fought my way through the crowd and reached the dressing rooms I looked

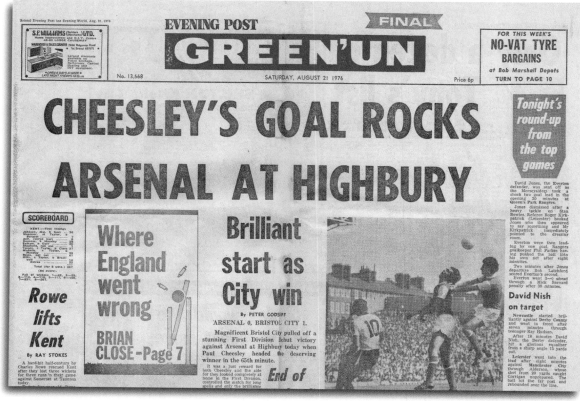

CHEESLEY'S GOAL ROCKS ARSENAL AT HIGHBURY

Tonight's round-up from the top games

SCOREBOARD

Where England went wrong

Rowe lifts Kent

By RAY STOKES

A hard-hit half-century by Charles Rowe rescued Kent after they lost three wickets for three runs in their first game against Somerset at Taunton today.

Brilliant start as City win

By PETER GODSIFF

ARSENAL 0, BRISTOL CITY 1.

Magnificent Bristol City pulled off a stunning First Division debut victory against Arsenal at Highbury today when Paul Cheesley headed the deserving winner in the 65th minute.

It was a just reward for both Cheesley and the side for they looked completely at home in the First Division, controlled the match for long spells and only the brilliance

BRIAN CLOSE—Page 7

End of

David Nish on target

as though I had gone five rounds with Mike Tyson! Then it was a case of where we were going to start the celebrations. A few of us partied a bit too much and it went on for days, so I can only apologise to the fans who paid to watch us against Notts County the following Saturday. But we were already up by then, so losing wasn't the end of the world.

Let's move on the first game of the following season against Arsenal at Highbury. It marked City's return to the top flight of English football after an absence of 65 years and you scored the only goal.

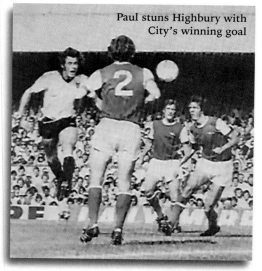

Paul stuns Highbury with City's winning goal

That was a fantastic day. It's a shame that some people seem to regard it as the only goal I ever scored for City, but it did prove to be the only one in the First Division. There was such a furore surrounding the club at that time and the M4 was packed with our fans making the journey to London. It was a really hot afternoon, which was great for the supporters, but not the players. I probably lost about nine or ten pounds in weight, but it was worth it because we pulled off a wonderful result.

We still had the momentum from the promotion season and there was a huge collective

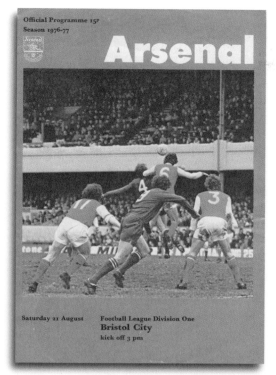

Official Programme 15P
Season 1976-77

Arsenal

Saturday 21 August   Football League Division One
Bristol City
kick off 3 pm

determination to show that we could compete at the top level. We weren't scared of anyone and the only point we had to prove was to ourselves, how good we were. That's exactly what we did on the day. My goal started with a Tom Ritchie break down the middle. When he was forced wide, he played the ball back to Clive Whitehead, who put in a fantastic cross for me to attack. I got a decent contact with my head, directing the ball downwards and just inside a post. Our fans were magnificent and the mood was that we were going to give a lot of the top clubs in the country problems. The lads did go on and have four fantastic years playing in the First Division, but unfortunately for me I didn't share that experience.

Just three nights later against Stoke City at Ashton Gate you suffered the injury that changed everything, competing in the air for a ball with Peter Shilton and landing awkwardly.

Yes, it was a bad injury. My leg straightened instead of bending naturally when I hit the ground and also twisted as a result. I chipped a bone in the knee as well as hyper-extending and ripping ligaments and cartilage. One side of the tendons was not good, but with the technology available these days there would probably have been a decent chance of recovery. It didn't help that I was running up and down the Dolman Stand each day in the weeks that followed before I was sent for x-rays and a proper diagnosis was made. That wasn't a great response by the club. Because I wasn't crying with pain, the feeling seemed to be that the problem was not serious, but I can assure you I was hurting. Back then, a lot of injuries to players' joints were treated with injections which, with the benefit of hindsight, we now know were detrimental to long-term health because they dried the joints out. Nowadays, clubs realise that players are such assets to them and worth so much money that they are taken out of games immediately there is a sign of an injury and given as much recovery time as they need.

You turned down the chance to play for England Under-23s towards the end of the promotion season because the game clashed with a City fixture and a lot of people think you would have gone on to play for the senior national team. Do you share that view?

It's not really for me to say. In fairness, I was going the right way at a time when England were short of centre-forwards. Paul Mariner went instead of me to the Under-23 game I was called up for and, with all due respect to him, I think I had a bit more in my locker

Time for celebration – manager Alan Dicks pours out the champagne for Paul at a dinner to celebrate promotion

than he did. Don't get me wrong because Paul went on to become a full international and had a great career, but at the time I thought I was as good or better and my career was progressing in the right direction.

It's well over 40 years since that memorable game against Portsmouth when you clinched promotion. Does it seem that long to you?
I can't think what I have been doing for 40-odd years besides getting up, going to work, and losing some hair. Thankfully, opportunities present themselves to get back together with the City boys of '76 and every time it happens it is a real pleasure. Of course, there are regrets over how my career ended, but nothing can take away the memories of that promotion season or the game at Arsenal that followed. They were wonderful days.

TERRY CONNOR

1991-1992

Already a vastly experienced striker at top level when joining City from Swansea City in 1991, Terry Connor soon picked up an injury, which effectively ended his Football League career. His first coaching job was under John Ward at Bristol Rovers and he later followed Ward to Ashton Gate, the pair leading City to promotion from the Second Division in 1997-98.

Tell us about your playing career prior to joining City.

I started off with my home-town club Leeds United, making my first team debut in 1979, and moved to Brighton in 1983 in a swap deal involving Andy Ritchie. After four seasons there, I joined Portsmouth where I stayed for three years and then I had just the one season at Swansea before arriving at Ashton Gate.

You scored a lot of goals for Brighton, in particular, where your form earned you an England Under-21 call-up. But it proved the briefest of international careers.

Yes, one game, one goal. At least I can claim a 100 per cent record! It couldn't have been a very good goal because I was never selected by England again. My one match was against Yugoslavia Under-21s in a qualifying tournament back in 1986.

Stuart Pearce and I played as over-age players. Also in the team were the likes of David Rocastle, God rest his soul, and Tony Adams from Arsenal, along with Nigel Clough. It was a great night for me. I scored a goal and thought I played well, but I was never invited back. The manager was Bobby Robson and when I saw him again many years later during his time at Newcastle United he still didn't remember my name!

Your hopes of doing well at Ashton Gate were dashed by injury early on. What happened?

It was just after my 29th birthday and I had only made around a dozen appearances for City. I was still finding my feet at the club and remember players like Gary Shelton, Andy May and Mark Aizlewood were very good in helping me to settle in. We played at home

to Charlton Athletic and in the very first minute of the game I was attempting to shield the ball to let it run out for a throw-in. I believe it was Scott Minto who came in and caught me on my left knee. My leg was trapped and I heard a kind of popping sound on the inside of the knee.

The great Buster Footman came on to treat me and I thought I was okay to carry on. But as I turned and put weight on my leg there was no ligament support there and I fell over again. Buster told me I had to come off and actually carried me around the pitch and down the tunnel without any assistance. I did try to come back from the injury, but only managed two or three games before consulting with Buster and a specialist and deciding I would have to bring my playing career in the League to a close.

You made the transition to coaching and your first job was at Bristol Rovers.

I had started off working in Rovers' school of excellence with Tony Gill. One evening we were taking the six to ten-year-olds and John Ward, who was manager at the time, came along to watch the session. After it had finished, he pulled me to one side and said how impressed he had been. A year later he was looking for a reserve team coach and invited me to take the job, working with him and Steve Cross. That enabled me to coach senior professionals for the first time and I really enjoyed the experience.

You have to get used to the fact that certain players will try to put one over on you and I learned a lot. To be fair, most of the Rovers lads were great, particularly players like Andy Tillson, who was a model pro. I started to understand what first team players required from a coach, as well as what the manager needed from them. I tried to be a go-between, a sort of bridge between the manager and players.

How soon after John Ward became City manager did you join him at Ashton Gate?

It would have been the following season, I think. By then Ian Holloway had taken over as Bristol Rovers manager, with Geoff Twentyman as his assistant, and I was operating under them. I learned a lot from that spell because John had worked in a different way and I found out that there was more than one approach to running a professional team. Ollie was a player-manager then, which meant he left a lot of the coaching duties to me,

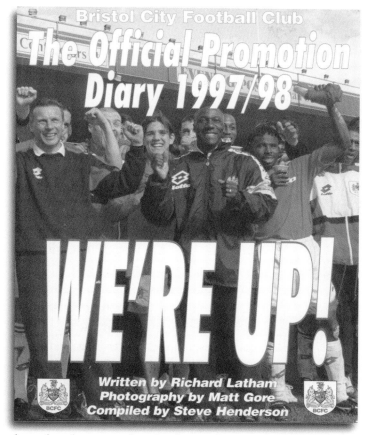

Bristol City Football Club
The Official Promotion Diary 1997/98
WE'RE UP!

Written by Richard Latham
Photography by Matt Gore
Compiled by Steve Henderson

and it was another important part of my learning curve. It meant that by the time I joined John at Bristol City I was a much more experienced coach.

Success came straight away for you on the red side of Bristol because City won promotion in your first season.

John Ward had already laid good foundations, taking the team from mid-table to the play-offs the previous season. He took a very good group of players and moulded them into a successful team. By the time we entered pre-season ahead of the 1997-98 campaign we were able to realistically challenge the players to achieve at least a top six finish. It proved a long hard season, but in the end we managed to go up in second place.

How were the coaching duties split between John Ward and yourself?

I would normally take the sessions on Monday to Wednesday, working with the players and looking to develop lads like Matt Hewlett and Tommy Doherty, who were just graduating from the reserves into the first team. It was great for me to work with players of such potential and try to teach them things that would help sustain their performances throughout the season. Then there were the experienced players like Shaun Taylor, who just needed to keep things ticking over. Shaun Goater was forever wanting finishing sessions, so I worked a lot with him, while Colin Cramb had a similar attitude to improving his skills. John would take over on Thursdays and Fridays to work on team play and between us we got the squad prepared for a Saturday fixture.

You had three strikers competing for two places in Shaun Goater, Steve Torpey and Colin Cramb. Having formerly played in that position yourself, you must have particularly enjoyed working with them.

Yes, especially because they were all different. Steve was an old-fashioned number nine, Shaun a poacher inside the 18-yard box and Colin was a good all-round player, with a bit of flair about him, who could come short for the ball and turn defenders. They all made important contributions and I remember continually stressing to them that you can't have

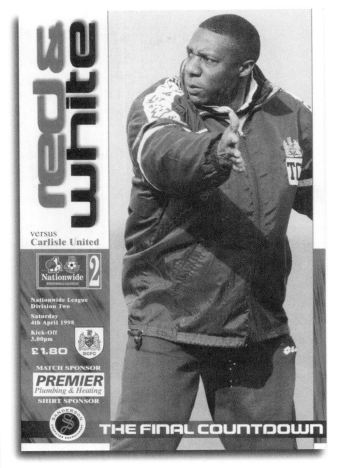

just two players filling the striking roles every week. There had to be competition for the places and each of them needed to be ready when asked to step up. Often one would be sat on the bench and then suddenly called upon to do his stuff. He had to be prepared mentally and physically to make an impact. They did it particularly well, which was a big part of our success. Late in the season we added Sean McCarthy and Jason Roberts to our options as loan signings after Shaun Goater was sold and they too made contributions.

The battle for the title was between Watford and City for much of the season. How disappointing was it to lose out in that duel?

We wanted to finish top and have a trophy to show for our efforts. But the achievement of winning promotion without having to be involved in the play-offs was great compensation. We had been running neck-and-neck with Watford over a long period. Both games between the teams were drawn, but in the end they probably just about deserved to pip us to the title.

Before the final home game of the promotion season against Walsall, you walked onto the pitch with John Ward and Buster Footman, linked arms and waved to the crowd. That must have been a special moment.

That was John's idea. We didn't have a lot of staff working us at the time and the three of us did most of the work. He wanted to give Buster and myself some recognition, so we all went out together and waved to the crowd. It had been a tough season, as well as a very rewarding one, and it was special celebrating with the fans, having clinched promotion with several games still to play.

It was a time of huge optimism at the club. Yet only six months later John Ward left to be replaced by Benny Lennartsson and City went on to finish bottom of the First Division?

I look back on that period with massive regret. With a little bit of stabilisation at the club, I am sure John and I could have kept the team progressing in the right direction. I am not claiming we would have reached the Premier League, but I do firmly believe the foundation was in place to build on what we had already achieved and become a force in what is now the Championship. Working with Benny Lennartsson was another learning experience for me. At the time I probably didn't appreciate it, but he was a very knowledgeable man. His problem was communicating that knowledge to the players. Looking back, I don't think he used me as his coach enough to overcome the language difficulty and get his messages across. Some of the players doubted what he was trying to do during his coaching sessions and his talks before games and at half-time. But I did learn from him and he was a clever man, who knew his football.

At the time of this interview, you are coach at Ipswich Town under Mick McCarthy, having been manager and coach at Wolves. What is life like for Terry Connor today?

Very much as it was when I was at Ashton Gate. I am always grateful to be in a job because football is such a precarious business and I work as hard as I can to make a success of whatever role I am in. I enjoy working with Mick and the staff we have at Ipswich and appreciate the opportunity to work with another group of good players. We have made good strides over the past three years and I just want to keep my head down, continue to work hard and enjoy being involved in the sport I love.

STEVE COTTERILL

Already an experienced manager with several League clubs, Steve Cotterill was appointed City boss in December 2013 and quickly transformed their fortunes, leading the Robins to promotion from League One in a memorable 2014-15 season, which also saw his team lift the Johnstone's Paint Trophy at Wembley.

What will be your abiding memories of the 2-0 Johnstone's Paint Trophy Final win over Walsall?

I always say to players that the best memories of days like that are the final whistle and the 30 or 40 minutes after the game because it takes you to a different level. You realise you have achieved something really special and the chances are it will have been either at Wembley or the Millennium Stadium. Winning the game is great, but it is that period immediately afterwards that sticks in your mind.

There was emotion before the start with six-year-old wheelchair-bound supporter Oskar Pycroft leading the team out.

I remember holding his hand just before the game and asking if he was okay because he was sat out there in front of a big crowd. But he seemed to be lapping it up and I think he enjoyed every moment.

There was a long gap between the Southern area final of the Johnstone's Paint Trophy and the final itself. Was that a problem for you?

Probably not, simply because of the number of games we had in between. I think it was something like seven weeks between beating Gillingham to get to Wembley and the final taking place, but that time actually flew by because of the number of times we were playing Saturday and then Tuesday in the League. It was relentless for us and it actually proved a good thing to have plenty of time before Wembley because there was a lot to organise. A great many people worked very hard behind the scenes, with things like tickets, car parking passes, where we were going to stay and where we would train, to make sure everything went as smoothly as possible on the weekend of the final. It was a real team effort and things did go very smoothly. From the time we left Ashton Gate, we knew what we would be doing virtually every hour leading up to the game. Preparation is something I am really strong about as a manager because it can make such a difference.

It is always billed as the 'Family Final'. How big a day was it for the Cotterill clan?

My family certainly enjoyed it as much as any other family. When you get to the stadium for a big game like a final you always worry about where they are and whether they are okay having been caught up in 70,000 people trying to enter the ground. My youngest daughter couldn't be there because she had to work, so that was a bit of a downer for her, but my eldest was up in the Royal Box and I was able to hand the trophy to her to hold up during the presentations.

You also saw your squad as a type of family and made every effort to get striker Matt Smith involved on the day, even though his loan spell from Fulham had ended earlier in the month.

Yes, I felt that was important. It must have been quite difficult for Matt to be with us again, having gone back to his parent club. I noticed since that in the photographs of the presentations and the champagne popping after the match he was in the background a bit. That was humble of him and really summed him up as a lad. None of the players had forgotten what he did for us during his loan. He came to see them on the Saturday night and then joined back up with us again the following day. It was great to see him and I am sure he will always be welcome at the club.

Team spirit is so important to you and, while some City squads over the years have been too big, yours is compact, with everyone playing a part.

We have kept a tight ship this season. Sometimes we have pushed our luck with it a bit if I'm totally honest because you never know when injuries will strike, but we managed to navigate our way through any difficulties in that respect. Having a smaller group of players can be a benefit, as long as you don't get too many injuries.

The important thing is to ensure the squad is balanced. If you go into a job as a manager where the team are struggling at the wrong end of the table, the chances are that the squad is unbalanced. I always like to ensure there are enough defenders in the camp because they have to work as a unit. You can take a striker on loan and get lucky with him, like we did with Matt Smith. But if you have to bring a defender in all of a sudden, is he going to be up to speed with what the other members of the back-line do? You need to be well stocked in what I call the bread and butter areas and that has been the case with us this season.

You have always said that the pre-season tour to Botswana was paramount in building team spirit. How confident were you back then that it would be a season to remember?

Not as confident as it has proved I should have been because it has gone so well for us. If I said I expected what has happened at the start of the season, I don't think people would believe me. And I would think the same if I saw myself on TV making that claim. I was always confident that I had a fully committed group of players because we had the right characters in the dressing room.

But for them all to blend in as quickly as they did and become team-mates, with the word 'mates' underlined, is all credit to them. That's not down to me. The boys who welcomed the new players into the club and those signings themselves have been responsible for being such a good fit.

It's fair to say the team clinched promotion in style with a 6-0 win at Bradford City. What do you recall of that night?

We had threatened to do that to opponents a couple of times earlier in the season without coming up with enough finishing touches. Against Bradford, everything went in for us. I would have been just as pleased with a 1-0 victory, but because it was so emphatic everyone wants to talk about it. It was certainly a nice way to win promotion, but I don't want to disrespect Bradford by making too much of it. It was a sore night for them and I am sure they don't want to be forever seeing Steve Cotterill crowing about it.

It was three points, a good win and promotion. We celebrated on the pitch afterwards with that cheap champagne they give you to splash about. I don't know if any of the lads took a swig or two, but there was no alcohol consumed after that because we had another game to prepare for. The main thought afterwards was to crack on and win the League One title. That's what I wanted more than anything and we were determined to stay grounded to achieve it.

The season has been entertaining, as well as successful. How important is it to you to win the right way?

We have tried throughout the season to play attractive football and when that hasn't proved possible, we have still managed to carve out some good results. Over the course of the campaign, some of the football we have played has been fantastic. The team now have an identity and the fans understand it. There are times when you need to slow things down in a game, rather than playing at 100 miles an hour.

When I first arrived, there were a lot of times when we played the ball along the back-line and used the goalkeeper to suck opponents into pressing us before moving it forward. The lads got edgy and so did the supporters, but now it is all part and parcel of how we play and the fans go with it. We got caught a couple of times last season against Wolves trying to play out from the back, but that is going to happen if you want to be a good footballing side.

If promotion was clinched in emphatic style, the same could be said about the finale to the title campaign, an 8-2 home win over Walsall. What a testament to the fitness alone of your squad to score six unanswered goals in the second half.

In the first half we weren't quite where I wanted us to be. It was the last game of the season and you don't want to add any blemish, but at times before the break we were sloppy. It's understandable. I dreaded it happening in the previous game because once you achieve something like clinching promotion there is always a comedown period. Against Walsall, it looked like affecting us.

We got our noses in front, but they deservedly got back to 2-2 and we needed to buck our ideas up. It was nothing major, but we had to be a little bit sharper and have the fire in our bellies that we had shown from day one. If we found that, I knew we would score more goals in the second half and that's what I told the lads at half-time. We were a lot better in the second half.

Jose Mourinho said this week that memories mean more to him than trophies. Do you understand what he means?

Absolutely. Jose is a winner, isn't he, so he knows. You enjoy trophies and have some fun with them at the time. It's great to see them in your club's boardroom and next season's team photograph. But the memories live longer. Football is a transitional sport, but it has been a special group of players that we have had this season and there will always be a special bond between us, even after we have left the club. That is certain after what we have all been through together.

Luke Freeman was among the nominations for League One Player-of-the-Year. How important has his contribution been?

Massive. That's the only word I can use. His assists have been first class, along with his goals, and his professionalism has improved. He is more aware of his diet than when he joined us and he is a young man who will continue maturing from year to year. It has been a big season for him and he has become a fantastic team player, whereas he was more of an individual at Stevenage, perhaps because he felt he had to be. As much as we have enjoyed his goals and assists, his simple passing and linking with the strikers has been just as important for us.

The squad is so tightly knit. Will you have to be particularly careful about the characters you add to it in the summer?

We were very careful about that last summer and it has paid off, so I don't foresee our recruitment policy being any different. The current group of players deserve to be going into the Championship because they have matured as men and footballers through the season, becoming very professional collectively. They are a fantastic group. When we left the Marriott Hotel at Preston, for example, the boss there came up to me and said what a credit the players were to the club. That has happened more than once this season and they really are top lads. We still have to find out how they will embrace Championship football. When you get promotion as a manager, you say to yourself this and that player will cope at the higher level, but until you get up there you don't know for certain. There isn't as much urgency to sign new players as there was last summer because now if you look around and think where do we strengthen, it is very difficult. We need to take a more measured view. The chances are that the players we look at will prove a bit more expensive than a year ago, so it might take longer to negotiate acceptable fees. As we speak, I have no idea of my budget, but I wouldn't expect the volume of signings we made in the build-up to this season.

It's often said about you that you eat, drink and sleep football. What do you do to relax on a rare day off or on holiday?
On the last day off I had, I walked to my local Costa and when I went through the door, I was told that my coffee was on the house, so that was a bonus. I then went for a walk in and out of some shops, nothing much more than that. I do try to take a break from football during summer holidays, although they don't mean a break from my phone. I like to get away overseas. Even then, I always tend to bump into someone who wants to talk about football. But that's okay. I don't mind it at all. At the end of a season like this one, it is important to have a break because it has been so relentless. But if it is relentless and successful, I am more than happy.

KEITH CURLE

1983-1987

After starting his career at Bristol Rovers and moving to Torquay United, Keith Curle joined City for £10,000 in 1984 as a winger. He was converted to centre-back by manager Terry Cooper to such effect that he went on to play for Reading, Wimbledon and Manchester City, gaining three full England caps. Later he became a successful coach and manager.

How did you become a professional footballer?

I was attending Oldbury Court Junior School and one of the teachers there, John Elliott, saw something in me that made him badger my mum to allow me to play for the school team. She was a single mum working as a manageress in a supermarket and had been through a bad time. She didn't want me out after school doing any activities whatsoever and getting into mischief, preferring me to be at home where she could keep an eye on me. Mr Elliott told her I had talent at football, but it took several visits to persuade her that he would act as a guardian, picking me up and dropping me back home after games.

I played in a seven-a-side competition at Longwell Green FC, where I first met my great pal Ian Holloway. I won an award for my performance in that competition and that got me scouted by Bristol City, who signed me as an associate schoolboy. I played for Knowle Boys and when I reached the age of 16, the time to be offered an apprenticeship, manager Alan Dicks told me that the opinion of the coaching staff was that I was not good enough to have a career with the club.

At the time, I thought I might become an athlete because I was a very quick runner. But my girlfriend of the time, Geraldine, who later became my wife, was able to help get me a trial with Bristol Rovers because her dad worked for Bristol and West Motor Auctions and they supplied sponsored cars for the then manager Terry Cooper and his assistant Clive Middlemass. I played at centre-forward as an over-age player in an Under-15 game and scored six or seven goals.

A week or two later, I was offered an apprenticeship and something like 18 months after that I scored on my first team debut against Chester at Eastville. Bobby Gould had given me my first professional contract and later signed me for Wimbledon.

31

Keith with his good friend Ian Holloway during their Bristol Rovers days

After playing 30-odd games for Rovers, you joined Torquay United for the princely sum of £5,000 before arriving at Ashton Gate.

Yes, David Williams was the manager who sold me to Torquay. He had two right wingers in myself and Ian Holloway. I got into the team before Ollie, but he worked tremendously hard to earn a place and when I suffered a knee injury, he took his chance. I couldn't get back into the side. I became disillusioned and I remember going to the Hollybush Pub in Bristol one night with Ian and Phil Kite and telling them football wasn't for me. I was training all week and there was only one substitute in those days, so I was hardly playing. That's how close I was to quitting before I went to Torquay. I tell people now never to be afraid to take what appears to be a step backwards because I scored on my debut for Torquay, went on to get half a dozen more goals, and resurrected my career. Within months Terry Cooper, who had moved to Bristol City, came in and signed me. But I will never forget Ian Holloway telling me that I didn't realise how lucky I was being a footballer and that I didn't want it badly enough. Those words stayed with me.

You went straight into the City team and two months later promotion was clinched from the old Fourth Division.

The only place I could get into the team was on the left wing because Howard Pritchard was established on the right. So, it was either that or be a squad player. People ask if it was difficult moving to City, having been with Rovers, but I never really bought into that rivalry thing. There were some fantastic characters in the City dressing room at the time and a great blend of youth and experience. Terry Cooper and Clive Middlemass didn't only put together a good team, but also a really honest group of players, who got on well. Rob Newman, who went on to have a great career, was still developing, and we had some brilliant characters, like big Trevor Morgan and Forbes Phillipson-Masters. After we won promotion, Terry added Bobby Hutchinson to the squad and his infectious personality brought us even closer together.

How did the switch to centre-back come about?

It felt really strange to start with and not natural to me at all. But Clive Middlemass later told me that after seeing me play at the back for only a few games, Terry Cooper predicted that I would play for England in my new position because of my exceptional pace. How incredible is that? As a former international player himself, Terry knew what a key asset it was to be quick. I owe a huge debt to Clive, who also saw something in me I didn't know I had and worked tirelessly to make me a better player. As a winger, I had been all right-footed, but in the later stages of my career my left was as good as my right. That was down to the time I spent with Clive in front of the turnstiles at Ashton Gate, striking the ball through one and then the next, all with my left foot. It was repetitive training, but it worked and I will always have a lot of time for Clive because he was prepared to invest his time and energy in developing me as a player.

The next big success was City reaching Wembley for the first time. What do you remember of the victory over Bolton Wanderers in the 1986 Freight Rover Trophy final?

Funnily enough, my most vivid memory was being absolutely flattened by Asa Hartford, the Scottish international Bolton had playing in midfield. I had gone past someone and was stretching my legs looking to take the ball forward out of defence when he completely wiped me out. The occasion was a bit surreal. My mum was in the crowd and it was probably her proudest day, seeing her son play at Wembley. But there was a game to be played and I was so focussed on that. I didn't really take everything else in. I don't even remember my ball into the box, which led to the opening goal. Looking back now, I wish I had taken more photos or kept a video because it was a very special day. Only years later did it really sink in how amazing it was. I had been brought up at Downend and lived at Pucklechurch, so as a proud Bristolian, it was extra special for me. When the players occasionally reunite, it reminds me of what the spirit was like back then and how a football club changing room should be. There was a lot of honesty and ability in that squad, but a lot of good humour too. As a manager, I have tried to install the same foundations at the clubs I have worked for. The environment has to be right.

Keith in Wembley action during the 1987 Freight Rover Trophy final against Mansfield Town

What was Terry Cooper like as a manager?

Both Terry and Clive Middlemass treated us as adults and were respectful to us, offering words of advice when they felt it necessary. Both had a deep knowledge of the game and I learned so much from them. But if you did something wrong, they would let you know in no uncertain terms. After one home game Terry threw a cup of tea at me and I still remember the reason. I had gone for a header that I shouldn't

EVENING POST, WEDNESDAY, MARCH 5, 1986 — 43

Oh boy! Keith caps dream days

By Richard Latham

CITY 3, NEWPORT 1

KEITH Curle's memorable last minute goal completed the happiest two days of his life.

At nine o'clock on Monday morning Curle's wife, Geraldine, gave birth to their first child — a boy named Thomas — and since then the 22-year-old City defender has been walking on air.

Perhaps that explains how he managed to glide 70 yards from inside his own half to score with a superb solo effort which will be the talk of Ashton Gate for the rest of the season.

With battling Newport pressing for a second equaliser, Curle's blistering pace took him past

the advantage. Seven minutes after the interval their defence was split wide open by a Gordon Staniforth pass which presented Steve Mardenborough with a simple equaliser.

The goal enabled Newport to persevere with the sweeper system and City's superiority had vanished by the time Steve Johnson replaced the injured Bobby Hutchinson after 68 minutes.

Johnson found it hard to get into the game. But

Bristol City's Bobby Hutchinson slides into a tackle against Newport, at Ashton Gate. Picture by Terry Dite.

Challenge answered

TERRY Cooper threw down an unusual challenge to his team at half-time.

CITY VIEW

have and failed to make contact. When Terry challenged me about it, I said: "I thought I would try to win the ball." The next thing, a cup has come flying past my ear, accompanied by the words: "Next time, don't think, just do as you are told." I didn't lose many headers after that!

You didn't score many goals for City, but one against Newport County at Ashton Gate in 1986 must rank among the best ever scored at the ground.

I will always remember it because a couple of days earlier Geraldine had given birth to our son Thomas. I was adamant that I wanted to play in the game, even though I had spent a fair bit of time away from Ashton Gate looking after mother and baby. I had a real buzz about me before kick-off and can still picture the goal now. I picked up the ball at the back and, as

Keith challenges Liverpool's Ian Rush during a pre-season friendly at Ashton Gate

I moved forward, space just seemed to open up in front of me. I got further and further upfield until I only had the goalkeeper in front of me. It was then that I realised why I wasn't a centre-forward because I didn't have a trick in me to go past him. I had no option but to shoot and, if I'm honest, I think the ball took a slight deflection before going in.

Your first big-money move was to Reading, but it was at Wimbledon that you really came to prominence. What was life like with the 'Crazy Gang'?

On my first day there a five-a-side game was arranged. As I was completing my medical, John Fashanu walked in and asked me which team I was playing for. I said: "I don't know" because I had no idea what he was talking about. It was only when I got outside that I realised one of the sides was made up of white players and the other non-whites. I was mixed race, so I could have played for either. In the end I opted to join the black lads and, let me tell, you it was a good decision because that was one competitive team! Happily, times have moved on and that wouldn't happen at clubs anymore. Wimbledon had just won the FA Cup under Bobby Gould and were looking to cash in by selling their best players. There was some in-fighting over who was going to be the next captain because there were still some experienced players there, such as Fashanu, Dennis Wise, Lawrie Sanchez and Vinnie Jones.

Bobby Gould had just paid £500,000 for me and, at our first meeting after I signed, he told me he was going to make me captain. My reaction was that it was going to be hard enough for me to concentrate on my own game at a higher level, but Bob insisted it would be a great challenge and finally I accepted. He was right about it being a challenge with that particular group of players. They were demanding. If things weren't right, everything went through the captain and it was me who had to go and see the manager. I had a great relationship with Bob, who didn't want confrontation and knew I wasn't a confrontational person. Being integrated into the group as captain was hugely testing, but it stood me in good stead for the remainder of my career.

Then came the really big move of your career, a £2.5 million transfer to Manchester City.

Sam Hammam, the Wimbledon chairman, didn't want me to go. That was because he knew that the longer he kept me, the better I was playing and the more money he could demand for me. In the end, I had to fall out with the club to get my move. Bobby Gould had left and Ray Harford was the manager. I made the point that I was playing in front of 5,000 crowds for Wimbledon at Plough Lane and, as much as I loved that, a move to the likes of Manchester City was what I had worked for throughout my career to date. It was a phenomenal deal for Wimbledon, who were making five times what they paid for me, and finally they agreed.

I travelled up to Maine Road full of excitement and then failed my medical. Having already met Peter Reid, the manager, and Peter Swales, the chairman, I was absolutely mortified. I was deemed to have an arthritic knee after a number of operations. I was sent for another medical and then to a specialist in Cambridge. It was the longest car journey of my life. I knew the specialist had all my x-rays and the moments before going in to see him I spent pacing the floor, with my hands sweating. He agreed that my knee looked dodgy, but we went through my playing record and fortunately I had missed very few games during my three years at Wimbledon. In the end, that swung it and the deal went through.

You were so successful at Manchester City that it wasn't long before England came calling. How did that come about?

Graham Taylor was England manager at the time. The previous summer I had been selected to go on a tour to Australia, New Zealand and Malaysia. After a 23-hour flight, no one wanted to go to bed, so the first training session was organised and within 15 minutes I broke my jaw. We were playing a five-a-side and David Batty, who was on my side, caught me with an elbow, It was meant to be a relaxing introduction to the training camp, but I ended up getting my jaw wired and they wanted to send me straight home. My response to that was to say it had taken me years to get amongst international players and I wouldn't go.

A year or 18 months later I was put on standby for the England squad ahead of the 1992 European Championships. A lot of players were forced to pull out for one reason or another and I think I was actually called into the squad because I could provide cover in several positions. After appearing in a couple of warm-up games, I was asked to play at right-back in England's opening match of Euro '92 against Denmark. Graham Taylor had actually wanted Tony Dorigo to play there, but he didn't fancy it because he was naturally left-footed. I would have played in goal if they had asked me. But, having been playing regularly for my club at centre-back, it didn't give me the best chance to shine.

In fact, all my England caps were earned out of position. In the other two games I played at left-back and sweeper. And when I played sweeper, it was behind Des Walker, who played so deep himself that I found myself almost standing on goalkeeper Nigel Martyn's toes! I was also competing for a place with really solid defenders like Tony Adams and Martin Keown. I would have played for England more, and in my best position, but for the injury in Australia. But there are no regrets. I have three caps, played in the European Championships and learned a lot being part of the international scene.

Your success as a manager has come in the lower divisions. You must have aspired at some time to work at top level.

I still have those aspirations and I think I will achieve them. I have coached and been an assistant-manager under Neil Warnock at Queens Park Rangers and Crystal Palace. At QPR we got into the Premier League and when we lost our jobs we were not in the bottom three. I also got to a Play-off final with Neil, but when he went to Leeds United, I opted to try and make it as a manager myself, with the opportunity to go to Notts County. That wasn't just because I was doing all the work and Neil was taking all the money (only joking Neil). He had given me a lot of responsibility when I worked with him, but I wanted to be the one making the decisions on matchdays. As we speak, I am manager at Northampton Town, who are a club with a healthy budget and some good players, looking to me to put them at the right end of the League Two table. Hopefully, I can give them a new direction by reorganising and restructuring, as I did during my spell at Carlisle United.

BRISTOL'S
SUBS BENCH

JANTZEN DERRICK

After playing for Bristol Boys and England Schoolboys, Jantzen Derrick joined City straight from school and made his first team debut as a 16-year-old. Appearing mainly on the left wing, he soon established a reputation as one of the most skilful players to have donned a Robins shirt.

Jantzen is an unusual name for a Bedminster boy. Was there a special reason behind it?

My mum was with her sister in a sports shop when she was carrying me and, as they were browsing, she spotted the name Jantzen on a pair of swimming trunks. It was a well known swimwear brand in America and she took a liking to the name, which is how I got it. It could have been worse. She could have called me Speedo!

Tell us about your early football before joining City.

I played for my school, a little club called Ashton Wanderers and a very successful Bristol Boys team, who won the national cup against Swansea in a two-legged affair. A crowd of more than 20,000 watched the first leg at Ashton Gate where we won quite comfortably. Then we went to the Vetch Field at Swansea and were losing early on before recovering to win 4-3. I managed to get into the England Schoolboys side in 1958 and it turned out that five of the players I lined up with went on to become professionals, including Terry Venables, Ron Harris's brother Alan and my City colleague Adrian Williams. It was when I left school at the age of 15 that I signed at Ashton Gate and went onto the ground staff, which later became the apprentices, for two years.

It didn't take long for you to make your City debut.

No, that came away at Lincoln City in November 1959 and at the time I was the youngest player ever to play League football for City. I played quite a few games in the Second Division that season. My first manager was Peter Doherty, but he didn't stay in the job long after my debut because we were relegated and, after Les Bardsley took charge for a short spell, Fred Ford was appointed. As well as playing, I was doing all the jobs

apprentices were expected to do, like cleaning the stands and the dressing rooms and looking after the boots of the full-time professionals. In those days they had leather studs, which were banged in with nails, and we had to ensure that was done, as well as keeping them clean. I loved every minute of it because I lived by the ground and it was always my ambition to pull on the red and white shirt.

While everyone came to appreciate your skills, there was also criticism that you were not brave or consistent enough. Was that fair?

I suppose it was. My fighting weight was only ten stone and there were some big, ugly players in opposing teams at the time. The rules were not as restrictive on tackling as they are today and I got kicked a lot. Back then, I would say you had labourers and craftsmen in football teams and, without sounding arrogant, I was definitely the latter. Wingers are expected to do something positive with the ball when they get it and go past full-backs, rather than make a simple pass.

It is not easy to do that match after match, particularly if the team are not playing well and you find yourself isolated. If you try something and make a cock-up, the fans are on to you straight away. I may have had two good games in every three. When I think back now, I probably didn't fulfil my full potential. On the ball I was a good player, but if I had my time again, I would have tried to be a midfielder, rather than a winger because I could see a pass early and would have been involved in games more.

Who were the big players in the City team of that era?

One of the best I ever played with was John Atyeo, who was phenomenal. He was over six-foot-tall and very good in the air, but he also had a lot of skill for a big guy and was very cool in front of goal. I knew where John was going to be when I got the ball out wide. It wasn't rocket science and if I produced a decent cross, there was a good chance he would get on the end of it. He lived at Dilton Marsh, near Warminster, and drove to the ground every day. Every year he would get a new Hillman car – I think it was a Hawk or a Hunter – but he wouldn't pay the extra to have a heater fitted so he used to arrive wearing a big, heavy coat and scarf. It's fair to say he was careful with money, but he was a great guy and I loved him dearly.

We had a decent team in the Third Division after being relegated and managed to win promotion back to what is now the Championship in the mid 1960s.

One thing missing from Bristol football in recent years has been local derbies. But you must have played in many.

There was at least one every year because back then the Gloucestershire Cup final was played annually between City and Rovers and it was a major game for both clubs and the supporters. I remember watching one at Ashton Gate at the age of around 14, which Rovers won. But during my playing career we beat them more often than they beat us. There were a lot of local players in both sides, which ensured they were blood and thunder games. But off the field we socialised with the Rovers lads and I even worked with a quite a few. The wage structure in football when I started was very different to today. If you were paid £12 a week during the season, you dropped to £8 in the summer break and also lost the opportunity to earn win bonuses. So, we used to get jobs outside the game for five or six weeks in the summer. These days I watch City a lot, rarely missing a home game, and it makes me smile to see the players' cars lined up outside the stadium. My first car at the age of 17 was a 1936 Ford 8. Most of the players travelled to the ground by bus.

Who were the best players you came up against?

The best I watched and played against was probably John Charles, who was an absolute colossus at either centre-half or centre-forward. I remember the first time I saw him play was when I was in my early teens and he played at Ashton Gate for Leeds United. He started at centre-half that day and, if memory serves me right, they switched him to centre-forward in the second half and he scored the only goal of the game. I also had the privilege of being

Jantzen eludes Bristol Rovers legend Harold Jarman to get in a cross during a City v Rovers derby

in the same side as George Best in a charity game back in the 1970s. Bridgwater Town were bankrupt and a match was arranged to raise funds to keep the club going. George arrived with girlfriend Mary Stavin, a former Miss World, and was brilliant on the day, signing all the autographs and chatting with people. He seemed a lovely guy and he did what he had to do in the game, scoring a couple of goals and making some mesmerising runs, which I could only stand back and admire.

When your City career ended you went to France to join Paris St Germain. How did that come about?

I was made redundant by City when Alan Dicks was manager, so I was open to offers. I had a phone call from Arsenal, who had a close relationship with Paris St Germain, which still exists. Prior to that the relationship was with Racing Club of Paris, but they folded. Paris St Germain had only just been formed and asked Arsenal to recommend some players capable of doing well in the French First Division. My name cropped up and I went over to France to speak to them. They offered me a deal and I moved across the channel, staying first in an hotel and then a flat where my wife and children joined me at Christmas time. It was in a lovely area and I enjoyed my season over there.

The standard of football was very good and the French were a bit ahead of us in terms of nutrition and what food to eat before games. The training was different. During my time at City, footballs were considered expensive items, but Paris St Germain gave every player his own ball with his name on to train with. Concentration was on the skill factor, which suited me, but I found there were lots of players over there as skilful or more so than me.

More recently, the club contacted me, initially via Facebook, concerning their 50th anniversary celebrations in 2020. They had arranged for their women's team to have a game over here against Arsenal's women's team and wanted to send someone to interview me at my home as the first English player they ever signed. Later the likes of Ray Wilkins and David Beckham joined them, but I was the first and in some ways a bit of a pioneer because it was far more unusual back then for our players to sign for foreign clubs.

How good a player would you have been on the type of surfaces professional teams get to play on today?

I would have enjoyed it. When I was playing there were only two or three grounds I looked forward to visiting. One was Ipswich and another Middlesbrough. But if you watch film of football in the Sixties you will get an idea of how awful the pitches were. The game has advanced in so many ways. Players wear vests that allow coaches on the touchline to monitor how much ground they cover and whether their energy is flagging, or their sugar levels are low. I wouldn't have fancied that so much!

Marina Dolman MBE

As wife of long-serving City chairman Harry Dolman, club president Marina Dolman first attended games at Ashton Gate in the early 1960s. Over the 60 years since then, she has become as revered by supporters as her late husband and a fantastic ambassador for the club. She was made an MBE for services to football in 2017.

When did your association with Bristol City first start?

It began when I married Harry, which was in 1961, and he was chairman of the club. To start with, I thought I was going to get my Saturdays free, but he asked me to accompany him to football because it played such a big part in his life. Ladies were just starting to attend matches and he wanted me to look after the directors' wives. In those days, they had to use a separate room to the men and were not allowed in the boardroom at all.

What was Harry like as a chairman and a man?

As chairman, he was very strong, which applied to everything he did in life. But people could go against him and he would listen and often change his mind if he felt they had a valid point. I am biased when it comes to talking about him as a man because I loved him, but he was great fun. He loved people and he had the most wonderful common sense of anyone I have ever known. I still miss that. Whenever I am worried about something, I ask myself what Harry would tell me to do. I take a step back, think for a few minutes, and then I know exactly what his advice would be.

The Dolman Stand is a lasting tribute to Harry. It must give you a lot of pleasure when you watch games at Ashton Gate.

Every time I attend a home match, I look at the Dolman Stand and remember how hard it was for Harry to get it built. At the time most of the supporters and directors felt the money should have been spent on the team, rather than the ground. He always felt that the team and the ground should grow together and he stuck to that opinion very strongly. One of my memories of the days when the stand was being erected is very vivid. I had bought Harry a new suit, which was made of silk and mohair, for his

John Atyeo polishing his boots, watched by daughters Carol and Julie

birthday. It was a beautiful suit and I was very proud of it. He wore it when he was president of the Chamber of Commerce and one day he decided to wear it to a lunch. On the way, he stopped off at Ashton Gate to see how work on the Dolman Stand was progressing. He climbed over some seats and promptly made a three-quarter tear in a knee of the trousers. He stuck it together with Sellotape and went on to the lunch!

Harry put a lot of money into the club and was responsible for keeping it going through some hard times.
I think it is fair to say that. I don't know too much about it because it happened before we were married, but I know he handed over a large sum of money when it was desperately needed. The club was his true hobby and real love. He always wanted the team to do well and, during the time he was chairman, Bristol City played a part in every day of our lives. I liked football before we were married because my father was a very keen sportsman, so I knew a little about both Bristol clubs. But not that much. I had heard of John Atyeo and Arnie Rodgers, but that was the extent of my City knowledge.

You would have seen John Atyeo play many times. Was he the best player you have watched in a City shirt?
Yes. John was a wonderful player. He was 6ft 2ins and the thing I admired most about him was that he could turn on a sixpence. He was so light on his feet for a big man and I'll never forget the goal he scored against Oldham Athletic at Ashton Gate to clinch promotion at the end of the

1964-65 season. He received the ball with his back to goal on the edge of the penalty area and swivelled to knock it straight into the net. It was one of the best goals I have ever seen.

No one has to be in your house long to realise the City connection. Not least because of a striking portrait of Harry on one of the walls.

Not every portrait you see looks like the person being painted, but that is a wonderful one because it is such a likeness. Over the years, I have been given a lot of City memorabilia. People bring me all kinds of things, which is so kind of them and shows how much they love the club. Since I have been president, I have received a medal each time we are promoted, which is also very nice.

The Masters . . .

. . . of Ashton Gate. Chairman Harry Dolman and manager Fred Ford take a walk around the ground

You mentioned the promotion season of 1964-65, which has to be up there with your fondest memories.

Oh definitely. That was a marvellous team. Do you remember Mike Thresher? He was a great full-back. I never actually saw this, but I was told that when Bristol City played Blackpool at Ashton Gate in the FA Cup and Stanley Matthews was in the opposition team, Mike ensured he never had a kick. That says everything about him.

The manager of the promotion side was Fred Ford and he was a wonderful man. He loved football through and through. It was while Fred was manager that I travelled on the team coach for the first time. That was most unusual back then because women were not allowed on the coach with the players, but I was the only lady who went to the away matches at the time and Fred said it would be okay.

Harry told me to sit still and not talk to anyone, so that's what I intended to do. If I remember rightly, the game was at Bournemouth and we had only got as far as Newton St Loe when I wanted to spend a penny. I told Harry and his response was "Nonsense! Control yourself."

So, to my horror, I had to sit wriggling in my seat until we got to Warminster when dear Fred walked up the coach and said: "Are you alright, Mrs Dolman?" I answered: "No, Fred, I am desperate for the loo." He told me he would get the coach to stop at the next pub and luckily Harry had gone to talk to the other directors, so he didn't hear. I

breathed a sigh of relief and when we got to the pub Fred stood up and said: "Anyone who needs to get off can do so." I was the only one to respond so you can imagine how I felt. I don't know which of us was more embarrassed, Harry or me.

Harry's dream was to see Bristol City playing in the First Division and happily he lived to see it happen in 1976.

Harry always felt responsible for Alan Dicks because he had recruited him as manager from Coventry City in 1967 after recommendations from Jimmy Hill, who Alan had worked under at Coventry, and their chairman Derrick Robbins. The years after that were a struggle for survival in the Second Division, but Harry had faith in Alan and, of course, in those days managers were given longer to achieve success. Then came that amazing night of April 20th 1976 when we beat Portsmouth to clinch promotion. I will never forget it. I remember that the Portsmouth chairman, a man named John Deacon, was heartbroken because they were going down, while we were on the verge of moving in the opposite direction. I don't recall a lot about the game, but at the following match against Notts County a few days later Harry received a tremendous ovation from the supporters when he went up into the stand. By then, he had just become president of the club and it did so much for his morale because he had been ill. There was spontaneous applause when he appeared before the fans and it meant the world to him.

What do you remember of the First Division days?

Very little, to be honest, because Harry was ill and subsequently died during that period. One thing I do recall is driving him to the first match of the season following promotion at Arsenal. We won 1-0 and Harry was just delighted to be there and see his dream fulfilled. So much work over so many years had gone into it. From the time he died, I have been asked by every successive board to keep my seat in the directors' box, which is very nice. But I didn't go to away games for a while, so I didn't see as much of the team as before or since.

You have experienced good and bad times at Ashton Gate. Knowing you, I am sure you felt terrible about the sacrifice of the 'Ashton Eight' in 1982.
That was very sad and I remember shedding tears. The strange thing is that Harry had forecast what happened just before he died. He said to me: "If the club continues in the way it is going, in five years' time it won't be here." It was exactly five years later that all the financial problems came to a head and those eight players were put in an impossible position. What they did should never be forgotten and nor should the efforts of Ken Sage and Deryn Coller, who came forward initially with the rescue plan to keep Bristol City in existence. Des Williams became chairman and did a wonderful job, while the lovely Terry Cooper gradually turned results around on the pitch.

That brings us to 1986 and another unforgettable day when a Bristol City team walked out at Wembley for the first time. It must have been so special.
I went to the Freight Rover Trophy final against Bolton Wanderers as a guest of Des

Marina Dolman proudly wearing her MBE for services to football

Williams because his wife Dora was away on a pre-arranged family holiday. I remember just sitting there and thinking "how wonderful" because every time Harry and I had attended a big game at Wembley – and we had been to most of the FA Cup finals – he used to say to me "What I would give to see Bristol City walking out on this pitch". There I was, watching it for him. The team played so well and I was very happy for Terry Cooper because he made everything such great fun. He knew football inside out, having played for England, and worked so hard to lift the club after the trials of 1982.

Mention of England brings us to the fact that you were at Wembley on English football's greatest day, the 1966 World Cup final against West Germany.
Harry and I were invited to the final as special guests of the Bristol Rovers board, would you believe? Bert Tann, who was Rovers manager at the time, was also secretary of the

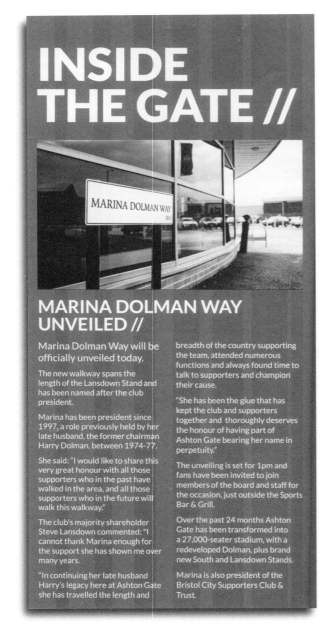

INSIDE THE GATE //

MARINA DOLMAN WAY UNVEILED //

Marina Dolman Way will be officially unveiled today.

The new walkway spans the length of the Lansdown Stand and has been named after the club president.

Marina has been president since 1997, a role previously held by her late husband, the former chairman Harry Dolman, between 1974-77.

She said: "I would like to share this very great honour with all those supporters who in the past have walked in the area, and all those supporters who in the future will walk this walkway."

The club's majority shareholder Steve Lansdown commented: "I cannot thank Marina enough for the support she has shown me over many years.

"In continuing her late husband Harry's legacy here at Ashton Gate she has travelled the length and breadth of the country supporting the team, attended numerous functions and always found time to talk to supporters and champion their cause.

"She has been the glue that has kept the club and supporters together and thoroughly deserves the honour of having part of Ashton Gate bearing her name in perpetuity."

The unveiling is set for 1pm and fans have been invited to join members of the board and staff for the occasion, just outside the Sports Bar & Grill.

Over the past 24 months Ashton Gate has been transformed into a 27,000-seater stadium, with a redeveloped Dolman, plus brand new South and Lansdown Stands.

Marina is also president of the Bristol City Supporters Club & Trust.

Managers and Secretaries Association. He organised for us to have a lovely lunch in a marquee at Wembley because they didn't have the big dining facilities that were later introduced at the stadium. We had a wonderful day, but I could have killed Jack Charlton when he gave away that free kick that led to West Germany equalising at 2-2 with so little time remaining. Thankfully, Geoff Hurst's hat-trick made it even more memorable, winning after extra time. I was with a group of Bristol Rovers ladies, who were waving flags, and we all had tears streaming down our faces. It was just a wonderful experience.

Back to Bristol City and more promotions under Joe Jordan, John Ward, Gary Johnson and Steve Cotterill, which meant many more happy memories.

John Ward was a lovely man, but to be honest I have liked all the managers who have worked at the club since my association with it began. They have all been good men fundamentally. The season under Steve Cotterill was particularly marvellous because we won the Johnstone's Paint Trophy, as well as the League One title, which was tremendously exciting. I like to watch good football and the way the team played that year was exceptional. Since we have been in the Championship, the standard of entertainment has continued and, but for two or three matches, I have loved watching the games. There have been plenty of times when we played wonderful football without finding the back of the net.

How long have you been club president and how do you view the role?

I was made president in 1997, so as we speak it is just over 20 years ago. I see myself as a link between the supporters and the club. I like to keep the fans involved as much as possible and make them feel part of Bristol City because I see us all as members of one big family. We all suffer terribly when we don't win, as well as enjoying the good days.

The modern-day Harry Dolman has been Steve Lansdown, who has also been huge in developing the club.

I don't know what we would have done without Stephen and the wonderful thing is that he really loves the game and the club, as does his wife Maggie and their son Jon too. His enthusiasm is such that he never seems to let the down times affect him. I sometimes expect him to be downhearted after setbacks and he is quite the reverse. You can tell what a fighter he is and we are all so grateful for the fact that he has kept his interest going.

We now have 'Marina Dolman Way' at Ashton Gate. What was your reaction when you heard about that?

One of complete surprise. Unusually, I was speechless! I also had the pleasure of unveiling the John Atyeo statue at the ground and that was a marvellous experience because I had watched him play and remember him so fondly. When we went to Wembley for the second time in 1987 to face Mansfield Town, I drove John to the game. I think he was working for radio at the time and the board asked me to look after him. On the way back the exhaust pipe fell off my car and we were clattering along the motorway. Forever afterwards, John told people I had been trying to keep him from getting home.

You seem to have the ability to always see the funny side of things?

You have to, don't you. That's life. Football can be very painful at times, but we wouldn't follow it as we do, were it not great fun.

BRISTOL'S
SUBS BENCH

Rob Edwards

1991-1997

At the age of only 18, Rob Edwards cost City £135,000 when signing from Carlisle United in March 1991. It proved money well spent as Rob went on to make more than 250 appearances for the Robins in either defence or midfield and became a full Wales international.

You had to wait a while for your first team debut with City, despite having cost a six-figure fee. Why was that?

Although I had played 50 games for Carlisle from the age of 17, I was still very young when I signed at Ashton Gate in the last week before the transfer deadline. City were doing well in what is now the Championship at the time. The club were in seventh or eighth place, going for the play-offs, and home attendances were 16,000 or more. Manager Jimmy Lumsden recruited me for the future as a development player, rather than to play

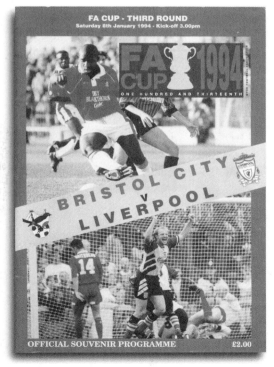

immediately. He put me in the reserves and I learned so much before making my debut the following season. Even then I only made about 15 first team appearances and it wasn't until the 1992-93 season that I had a decent run in the side. But I was fortunate joining a club with a lot of good, experienced players, who helped me as much as the manager and coaches

One of the highlights of your City career was being part of the team who knocked Liverpool out of the 1993-94 FA Cup at Anfield. What do you remember of that night?

We played really well and on the balance of play over three games, if you include the one abandoned through floodlight failure, we deserved to go through. I was a big Liverpool

fan and my mum comes from there, so it was a real thrill to play at Anfield. The Kop was still a standing area back then, which made it an even more thrilling experience. I had always wanted to play for Liverpool in front of those fans and I suppose winning in front of them for City was the next best thing. I had to try and avoid being star-struck because their team was packed with household names like John Barnes and Ian Rush. They were Liverpool legends and part of a team who had won a lot of trophies, so they were heroes to me.

By the time the 1997-98 season came around you were well established in the team. What are your recollections of that promotion season under John Ward?

John had come to the club in March of the previous season and took us to the play-offs, so we knew we had a good side. Shaun Goater was a top goalscorer and we were strong throughout the team. We didn't start the season well, but then went on an incredible run that took us to the top of the table. I still believe we should have won the Second Division title, but we ended up finishing runners-up to Watford when we probably had the stronger squad. That remains a regret, but the main objective was promotion. John Ward was great friends with Graham Taylor, the Watford boss, and it was nip and tuck between the two clubs who would finish higher. They were a good side, who went on to win promotion again the following season, but we got to the top of the table and didn't quite manage to stay there when we lost at Preston on the final day,

When City played Watford at Ashton Gate that season the match took place on a pitch with more lines than British Rail. And you scored in a 1-1 draw.

The pitch didn't look as good as it does today, that's for sure. A game of American football had been played on it a couple of days earlier and you could still see all the lines. It was crazy and disappointing when you consider that it was a showpiece game between the two best sides in the division. We didn't know whether to go for goals or touchdowns! On the day we just got on with it, but I don't think the current manager would be too impressed if it happened today. I remember being sent on as a substitute for Shaun Taylor, who suffered an injury in the first half. My forte was not going up for corners and free kicks and scoring goals like Shaun used to do. So I wasn't expecting it when John Ward waved me forward from the bench for a set-piece. He therefore took a lot of the credit for my goal. The ball was headed down into my path and I shot in from a couple of yards, which was about my range! I know it was two yards because there was a line on the pitch saying so! Having said that, I must tell you about my best goal. I actually scored for City past Peter Shilton, who was with Derby County at the time. We were 3-0 down and, believe it or not, I netted with a right-footed volley. Having searched for ages, I found film of it on YouTube to show my son.

Your appearances for City were split between defence and midfield. Which did you consider your best position?

I had played left-back for Carlisle, but I didn't do so for City until my later years at Ashton Gate. The six or seven different City managers I played for thought I could also do a job in midfield or central defence. Jimmy Lumsden was convinced I was a midfield player in the making when I arrived and I think I played my best football for the club under Russell Osman in the centre of midfield around the time we beat Liverpool. I had Brian Tinnion on the left of me and we had a number of good full-backs, capable of charging forward on the overlap. I really enjoyed that period in my career.

When your playing career finished you had a spell as manager at Tranmere Rovers and also spent a lot of time coaching.

I had eight years with Exeter City, four as a player and four as assistant manager, which bridged the gap and prepared me for a go at management. I spent six months in charge at Tranmere, which I really enjoyed. You don't know what it entails until you are the guy making all the decisions and I would like to have another go some time. But my real drive is to be as good as I can be as a coach, whether it is in senior football or youth development, which is of great interest to me. There is a real niche in the market for coaches who can bring the best out of young players because clubs focus so much on producing their own talent. My current employers are the Wales Football Association and I have a really nice role working with the Under-17 team, which is largely made up of first year scholars or apprentices, who have yet to make it in the professional game. We have players from all level of clubs from Manchester City down to non-League and we go and play against top nations, which exposes the boys to different styles of football. It is not all about winning, even though we want good results. It is more about making each boy better and able to move on to the higher age groups, then hopefully senior level.

From your experience at other clubs, how are Bristol City perceived by rivals around the country?

I think as a club that has underachieved when not in the Championship. My personal view is that City should at least be a side competing strongly in the second tier of English football and I believe that is reflected in how the club are regarded generally. There is no reason why they should not reach the Premier League, but in the past I think that has been attempted too quickly when it has been a realistic target. It has to be a four or five-year plan with gradual progress, rather than by big spending over a short period.

When we went up in 1997-98 everything seemed to be going in the right direction, yet we finished bottom the following season. The Championship is a tough league, as I found playing with City and Preston, and an awful lot of money is spent trying to reach the Premiership. For a club like City, it is all about building the necessary finances and facilities to accompany a strong group of players. I like what I see going on at Ashton Gate as we speak. The stadium is so different to when I was playing and the pitch is superb. The club have an excellent training ground and I am a bit envious because coaching these days is more technically based, which would have suited me.

That said, I wouldn't swap the era I played in because we had a lot of laughs and still do on the occasions we get together. I still live locally and get to watch City play whenever I can. My son is in Bristol Rovers' Academy, I have to admit, as an Under-14. He is a bit of both when it comes to being a defender or midfield player, a bit like his dad.

BUSTER FOOTMAN

It was in October 1988 that Joe Jordan recruited Harold 'Buster' Footman as City's new physiotherapist after the former Royal Marine had spent ten seasons in the same role at home-town club Southend United. Buster – the name was coined by an aunt when he was three days old – soon became an icon with fans and was awarded a testimonial by the club in 1999. He later served as kit-man.

Before you became involved in football you served in the Royal Marines. What effect did that have on your later life?

It was the making of me. I had experienced a difficult childhood due to chronic asthma, which people thought I would never recover from. I managed to get through it and joining the Royal Marines in 1956 opened up a whole new lease of life for me. Those Green Berets have to be earned the hard way, so I remain immensely proud of being able to wear one. The discipline instilled in me stayed with me forever and I saw parts of the world I would never have visited.

One sport you competed in during your time in the services was boxing. Tell us about that.

I boxed for the Navy first while I was in England and when I joined 45 Commando in Malta I boxed for the Army, winning the Malta Troops middleweight championship in 1957. I had joined local boxing and athletics clubs after my asthma was cured at the age of 15 to make up for lost time. The sporting side of service life was fantastic and I also represented my unit at football, cricket, rugby and hockey.

How did your career in football start?

I joined Southend in 1978 when their youth coach Frankie Banks invited me to help with his team and the reserves. My dad had been a trainer with the club and I was delighted to get the opportunity to follow him. One member of the youth side who made his first team debut while I was working with them was Glenn Pennyfather, who later played for Bristol City. I was appointed first team physio in 1983 when Brian

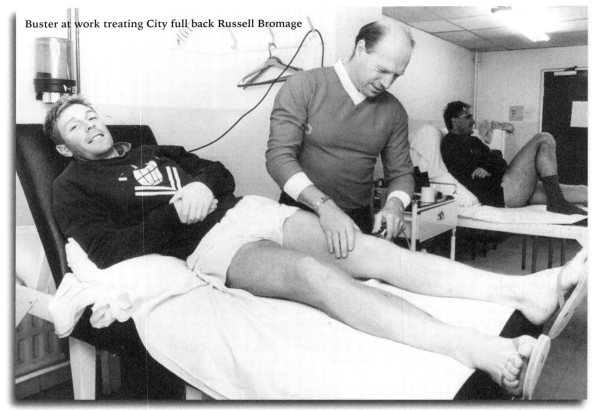

Buster at work treating City full back Russell Bromage

Beckett resigned. I owe him so much for the help and advice he gave me and I lost a good friend when he died in 1989.

During your time at Southend United, Bobby Moore was one of the managers. What do you recall of the man who led England to World Cup glory in 1966?

It was a privilege to have the chance to work with Bob. He was a wonderful man off the pitch as well as a great player. Everywhere we went he was mobbed by admirers. As a manager, he was very thorough with his preparation. If he had been in charge of Liverpool or Manchester United, he would have been more successful because he was used to dealing with top class players during his own career. Southend were in the Fourth Division at the time and he found it hard to fathom why the players couldn't do things that came naturally to him. They had to work that much harder to fulfil what he wanted from them.

How did your move to Ashton Gate come about?

I answered an advertisement for the job, but initially didn't get it. About a month later Joe Jordan contacted me to see if I was still interested. Southend had a game at Preston on the following Saturday and I told Joe that if there were no injuries I would come and see him on the Sunday. That's what happened. I didn't hesitate when he offerered me the job because I wanted a new challenge and it was the start of 16 wonderful years working for Bristol City. Joe took a chance on me and I had a lot of respect for him so it wasn't a difficult decision.

Buster in conversation with the manager who brought him to Ashon Gate, Joe Jordan

You were physio during two promotion seasons. Let's talk about the first in 1989-90.

That was a wonderful team. We had the run to the semi-finals of the League Cup the previous season and it was a great time to be at the club. I felt so lucky to be involved. Bob Taylor was scoring goals for fun and I am convinced we would have beaten Bristol Rovers to the Third Division title had he stayed fit. We had eight games to play when we beat Crewe Alexandra 4-1 at Ashton Gate and Bob scored a hat-trick. With us winning comfortably, Joe Jordan wanted to rest Bob and I had the number board in my hand to substitute him when he made a run out to the wing and pulled a hamstring. That was before the days when the fourth official held up the numbers. It was so unfortunate because, as things turned out, he played in only one of the last seven matches. But for that, he would have got 40 goals and we would have been champions, rather than Rovers.

Bob was a terrific player. I remember one game the following season when Jimmy Lumsden was manager and he was pondering on the bench whether to take him off. I told him: "Don't worry. Bob will score in a minute" and no sooner had I said it that he laced one into the top corner from 20 yards. Back then, I would be on the bench, with just the manager, his assistant and the two substitutes. Nowadays, there are so many sitting there that they need several rows of seats!

Another of your claims to fame is that you were City physio when the club played in Europe.

That was in the 1992-93 season when Denis Smith was manager and we played four games in the Anglo-Italian Cup. Two of them were at Ashton Gate, but we travelled to face first Pisa and then Cremonese. The Pisa trip was memorable because we were able to visit the Leaning Tower and the match itself was exciting, even though we lost 4-3. Andy Cole and Jacki Dziekanowski were in the side, while Leroy Rosenior was on the bench, so we had some fantastic individual players. We later drew 2-2 at Cremonese, with Andy and Leroy scoring, but overall the results were disappointing. Still, we saw some sites and it was European football.

Your second promotion season was working with manager John Ward and coach Terry Connor in 1997-98. The three of you were a close-knit team.

I had worked with John at Southend for a little while, so I was delighted when he was appointed manager. With Terry involved too, we just hit it off as a trio. We each worked off one another and it was another really enjoyable season. Shaun Goater was the Bob Taylor of that campaign. What a player he was. "Feed the Goat" he used to say and when we did he would stick the ball in the back of the net. Again we missed out on the title, this time to Watford, but promotion was the success we deserved because everyone worked so hard to achieve it. Before the last home game against Walsall, John got Terry and I together and insisted we all walked out together to salute the crowd. That was a wonderful moment for me.

There are not many physiotherapists who have been awarded testimonials by League clubs. But that's what happened to you in 1999.

Yes, I had wanted a pay-rise, but the chairman Scott Davidson offered me a testimonial year instead! I was up in the air for a few days and it turned out to be a wonderful 12 months, with a number of enjoyable events. Manchester United agreed to send an Under-21 team to play City at Ashton Gate in my benefit game and their side included Wes Brown, who was coming back from a cruciate ligament injury. It was really nice of him to take part, considering the future he had with United and England, and it reminded me of the goodwill that exists in football, which doesn't always get publicised. It puts a lump in your throat sometimes what people will do for you. We had an auction after the game and Andy Cole, who by then had long been a United star, sent a pair of his boots, signed and mounted, which raised a lot of money. I went home with a headache that night!

How has the treatment of players changed in the years since you retired?

Things have moved on so much in terms of the technology and emphasis on lifestyle. But one thing I don't like is the number of people now involved in a player's rehabilitation. In my time you had to work one-to-one because there was only the physio involved. And that meant building a trust with the player. He had to have confidence in you if he was going to apply himself properly to the business of getting fit. These days, one person will supervise the treatment, another the rehab, another the pressure work and so on. I don't think that is a good thing. I always knew how to deal with each individual player because I spent so much time with them. There were developments during my time in the job, one of the most important being the arthroscope, which meant keyhole surgery was possible on things like cartilage problems, which once kept players out for weeks. At Southend, I managed to get a lad called Stevie Phillips back playing after cartilage surgery in just ten days – and he scored. Before the arthroscope it was always touch and go with cartilage operations because there was a risk that a small bit of the cartilage would be left in the knee when the rest was pulled out.

Over your years in football you raised more than £100,000 for various charities. How did that start?

There was a school for disabled children in Southend and a group of the lads at the football club decided they would walk from Birmingham to Southend to raise money for it. I said I would join them and they all pulled out, one by one, until I was left to do it on my own. I enjoyed doing something to help the kids, so the next walk I did was Land's End to Southend. That took me ten days because it was 268 miles. It raised so much money and things just continued from there. Being employed in football, there were times when I could devote my energies to charity work, which I couldn't have done in a nine to five job. I did things like rowing and abseiling, raising money for old people, as well as children, and it gave me so much satisfaction.

The only thing I didn't do was a parachute jump. I went to do one, but bad weather intervened. A wonderful experience was climbing Mount Kilimanjaro when I was in my sixties to raise money for brain-injured children. I think it was 96 degrees at the start of the climb and minus 26 within three days as we approached the summit. I got to within 500 metres of the top and, although I still felt strong, I kept falling over because the altitude got to me. In the end, I was told I had to start back down, which was hugely frustrating. When I look back, I think I brought smiles to the faces of a lot of people, young and old, with the things my fund-raising provided for them and that gives me enormous pleasure.

BUSTER FOOTMAN RIP 1939-2020

We can't end without talking about your famed ability to wear a t-shirt on even the most freezing of matchdays. How did that come about?

No sense, no feeling mate, simple as that! That's what my mum used to tell me. You can't work properly as a physio wearing heavy clothes and being all cluttered up. It never bothered me wearing t-shirts because I didn't feel the cold. I never thought much about it, but to the fans it became my trademark. After I left Ashton Gate and was getting on in years, people would bump into me out shopping and ask why I was wearing a jacket.

How do you reflect on your career in football overall?

I have been a very lucky man. To do a job I loved, seven days a week, and get paid for it. You can't be luckier than that.

MIKE GIBSON

1963-1971

Rated by many the best goalkeeper in City's history, Mike Gibson joined the club from Shrewsbury in 1963 for the princely sum of £6,000. He went on to be an ever-present in the Robins' 1964-65 promotion season, helped them reach the League Cup semi-finals in 1970-71 and made 375 appearances before moving to Gillingham in 1972.

Where did football start for you?

I was born in Derby and played local football while I was at school. When I left I joined Gresley Rovers under former Derby County and England player Sammy Crooks before moving to West Bromwich Albion and playing in their youth team. Then I went up to Blackpool through Jack Nicholas, who was their scout in Derby, spent a week in lodgings there and took part in a practice match with some famous Blackpool names. George Farm was in goal, Stanley Matthews played and so did Stan Mortensen. Unfortunately, I got homesick and in any case my dad was not going to let me sign full-time or go on the ground staff because he felt I needed to serve an apprenticeship, which I did in engineering.

Burton Albion, then managed by another former Derby player, Jackie Stamps, came in for me and from there I joined Nuneaton Borough. By then I was about 20 and I finished my apprenticeship a year later. I was playing really well for Nuneaton and attracted interest from Shrewsbury, where yet another famous former player, Arthur Rowley, was in charge. When my apprenticeship ended, I moved to the town with a mate of mine from Derby called Peter Dolby. By a strange coincidence he later played at centre-half for Shrewsbury against Bristol City in two games over Easter where John Atyeo's goals helped us to the brink of clinching promotion in 1965. I wasn't with Shrewsbury all that long, but we reached the League Cup semi-finals against Rotherham United while I was there, which was quite an achievement.

You won an England Youth cap while at West Bromwich Albion. What do you remember of that?

It was against Switzerland at Brighton. It came about because I was playing for the senior Derbyshire XI and we had a match against Staffordshire. Dave Burnside was in the

Stafford team and I had one hell of a game that night. The next thing I know I am reading in the newspaper that an England scout had been there and I was selected for the international. It proved my one and only cap so I couldn't have done that well!

It was manager Fred Ford who brought you to Ashton Gate and word was he thought the £6,000 fee a bit steep!

I believe so. When I went back to Shrewsbury with City, Fred used to point to the new foyer they had built on the front of the ground and say the bricks had come from what he paid for me. It turned out to be a great move, although I didn't think so to start with, and by the 1964-65 season we had a team capable of beating anyone in the Third Division. There was Tony Ford and Alec Briggs at full-back, Jack Connor and Gordon Low, Lou Peters on one wing and Ray Savino on the other, Jantzen Derrick, and up front John Atyeo and Brian Clark. It was a super season, but I always remember Peter Godsiff, of the *Evening Post*, writing in our match programme after we lost a game 3-0 at Mansfield in March that our promotion chances had gone.

It was only two points for a win then and he felt we had too much ground to make up. From then on, we won virtually every game, including the two matches against Shrewsbury on successive nights. After that we had to beat Oldham Athletic at Ashton Gate in our last match and did so 2-0. If it was a coincidence that Pete Dolby played against us for Shrewsbury, there was another one in the Oldham game when John Atyeo came up against Alan Williams, a former team-mate with City.

The Oldham game is remembered not just for clinching promotion, but also as a kind of farewell to John Atyeo. What an occasion that must have been.

It certainly was. John was one of the best players of his day, simple as that. What he would be worth today. With Geoff Bradford over at the Rovers, we had two great strikers in Bristol at the same time. I played against John when I was at Shrewsbury and he scored a couple of goals past me. He was very intelligent as a footballer and as a man. Big clubs came courting him, but he was loyal to Bristol City. Of course, there wasn't the attraction of big money then, but he could certainly have played at a higher level. He felt a lot of loyalty to chairman Harry Dolman, who had first brought him to the club.

I don't know whether it is true or not, but someone told me the reason John didn't play more for England was because he didn't like flying. More likely it was because he was playing for a lower division team, but if so that was wrong. There were a lot of good England forwards at the time and, when you look at it that way, it's remarkable he got picked in the first place. But John was so strong on the pitch as well as skilful. I remember a game we played against Coventry City when they had a feared defence of hard-men, including George Curtis. John made a run towards a touchline with Curtis right up his backside and just at the last minute he stepped aside, sending Curtis crashing into the barriers. That was John. He didn't fear anyone.

Promotion 1965 – John Atyeo is mobbed by fans

The comradeship between the players in that promotion side was fantastic and there was also a close bond with the supporters. Fittingly, John scored the second goal against Oldham, which really sealed things for us. It was the only time I can remember getting drunk and then sober again on champagne! We went to the Town's Talk in Bristol where we were always well looked after and everyone was on cloud nine. Harry Dolman told Fred Ford he had a job for life! The following season we almost went up again from the Second Division, Southampton pipping us by just a few points. It was a major disappointment to get so close to Division One and results dipped after that.

Before every game at Ashton Gate you would run out towards the City fans at the East End and jump up to touch the crossbar.

That's right. I had a ritual and the main reason I did it was because it was a time of the old muddy pitches where the markings could be very faint and you could lose your bearings in the penalty area. I would leap to touch the crossbar, then measure out four yards from one of the posts to be precisely in the centre of the goal before moving forward to make a mark on the line of the six-yard box. In later years I did the same with the edge of the penalty area. Today the groundsmen wouldn't let me do it, but it isn't necessary anyway because the pitches are so much better and the lines can be clearly seen. The crowd got used to my routine and would cheer when I counted out my paces and touched the crossbar. Once a group of travelling City supporters at the bar after an away game asked me if I could do it on opposition grounds too. The routine actually helped me win the fans over in my early days at Ashton Gate. Yet at that time I was almost doing it subconsciously.

Another memorable season towards the end of your City career was 1970-71 when the team reached the League Cup semi-finals and faced Tottenham Hotspur.

It was the closest I came to a Wembley appearance, which would have been nice because I left the club shortly afterwards. We had played against Spurs and Jimmy Greaves in the 1966-67 FA Cup, but this time it was Alan Gilzean, who scored at Ashton Gate to stop us winning the first leg, which ended 1-1. Even then, the tie was far from over because we defended really well at White Hart Lane and took the game into extra time before losing 2-0, Martin Chivers getting one of the goals.

Since your playing career ended you have been goalkeeping coach at Ashton Gate and helped run a fitness centre at the ground, so your tie with City has remained solid.

As I said before, the move from Shrewsbury turned out to be brilliant for me. I came to love Bristol and have lived in the same house for more than 50 years. With playing, coaching, scouting the teams we were about to face and the keep-fit centre, I worked for Bristol City for close on 40 of those years and have so many wonderful memories.

CHRIS HONOR

1985-1989

Athletic defender Chris Honor emerged from the apprentice ranks at Ashton Gate to sign professional forms when Terry Cooper was manager in the mid-1980s. He went on to play in the League Cup semi-finals and was part of the 1989-90 promotion squad under Joe Jordan.

What do you remember about your City debut, which came at the end of the 1985-86 season away at Darlington?

My dad was a salesman at the time and did a lot of travelling, so you can imagine how pleased he was to have to hit the motorways again and go all the way to the North East to watch my first game. It was the last League game of the season – and the longest journey – but just around the corner was the Freight Rover Trophy final against Bolton Wanderers at Wembley. I was 17 at the time and one of many local lads in the reserves, so I was thrilled when Terry Cooper told me I was in the squad, having been very much a City fan as a boy.

My grandad, who lived to the age of 99, was a big supporter of the club and used to live on Smythe Road, near Ashton Gate. He made sure I never had any choice over which team I would play for if good enough, so Bristol City was in my blood. What I recall most about my debut is being given the run-around by Darlington's speedy winger and the whole experience going by so quickly. But I must have enjoyed it because I kept the shirt and it is still in my attic somewhere.

Did you go to Wembley for the Freight Rover final nine days later?

Yes, I did. If there had been five or more subs allowed back then I might even have been on the bench, but instead I watched proudly from the among the crowd as a supporter. Andy Llewellyn was a couple of years older than me, but we had grown up together at the club so I really felt for him when Terry Cooper didn't put him on as a sub in the closing stages. But at least he got to play at Wembley against Mansfield Town a year later, whereas I broke my leg that season and it was many more years before I managed to play there with Forest Green Rovers in the FA Trophy final.

You were in the City team by the later stages of the run to the semi-finals of the League Cup in 1988-89. What do you recall of those days?

I had not long been in the side when we played at Bradford City in the quarter-finals, so that was a fantastic experience, with Alan Walsh getting our winning goal, and I managed to keep my place for the two semi-final games against Nottingham Forest. Manager Joe Jordan was very meticulous, bringing a lot of ideas from Italy where he had played, emphasising the need to train properly and have the right nutrition. He put a lot of planning into every game to make sure we were as well-prepared as possible and took us to Nottingham well in advance of the first leg.

We stayed at Derby and everything was going fine until we made what should have been the half hour journey to the ground. I think we left the hotel at around 5pm, but with 8,000 City fans making the journey at rush-hour time it didn't prove early enough and I think we arrived at about 7.30pm for the 7.45pm kick-off. I remember watching goalkeeper Keith Waugh doing his stretches on the team coach and Joe telling us there would not be time for a warm-up on the pitch.

We literally ran into the dressing rooms, grabbing items of kit, There was no time to use the toilets, but also no time to get nervous, which for me as one of the younger players, was probably a good thing. Sometimes you can over-think things. I clearly remember walking out onto the pitch and being absolutely gobsmacked by the number of City fans in the stadium. It was an incredible sight and one of the great moments of my career.

The game ended in a 1-1 draw, which was an incredible effort by a Third Division side, against one of the best teams in the country.

Yes, the Forest team was so full of internationals that years later I remember their line-up

Bristol City FC, 1988/89: back row, l to r: Carl Shutt, Russell Bromage, Steve McClaren, Tony Caldwell. Middle row: Jimmy Lumsden (assistant manager), Alan Walsh, Rob Newman, Paul Fitzpatrick, Keith Waugh, John Pender, Paul Mardon, Glenn Humphries, Alan Crawford (youth coach). Front row: Nigel Hawkins, Ralph Milne, Steve Galliers, Joe Jordan (manager), Chris Honor, Andy Llewellyn, Mark Cooper.

better than our own. The likes of Stuart Pearce, Neil Webb, Steve Hodge and Nigel Clough had England caps and even those who weren't senior internationals, such as Franz Carr, were household names. My job was to keep an eye on Garry Parker, who unfortunately ended up scoring the extra time winner in the second leg, but in the first game we all did our jobs and somehow managed to come away with a draw.

Paul Mardon, who was my room-mate and the only player in the side younger than me, scored an amazing goal to put us in front. He never even scored in training. In fact, most of his shots went over the hedge and onto the road! I was about to shout "Don't shoot" when the ball came his way in the 65th minute, but somehow it ended up in the back of the net.

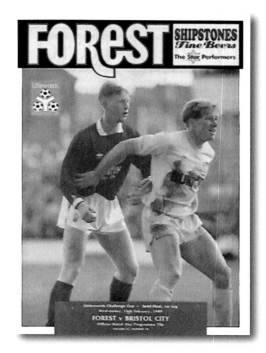

Mards had a great game overall. He had been given the task of stopping Hodge making his forward runs from midfield and was such a good athlete that he tracked Steve all over the pitch for every minute of the match. We were so close to winning when John Pender, one of the nicest guys I ever played with, scored that infamous own goal. He was always the one who would put an arm around you in training if you did something wrong and provide a few wise words.

When his interception sent the ball trickling into our net, with Keith Waugh wrong-footed, I could hardly believe it. There was a moment's hush as it rolled over the line, then the ground erupted. In the end the goal proved crucial because we held Forest again over 90 minutes at Ashton Gate in the second leg and, had we won at the City Ground, would have gone to Wembley.

That second leg was played in foul weather. Alan Walsh hit a post in the final minute of normal time before Garry Parker's winner, which must have made losing even more devastating.

It was such an outstanding effort by our players over the two games that I was inconsolable when we lost. Pitches these days are so pristine, but back then the sort of rain that fell in Bristol ahead of the second leg made them so heavy and demanded that much more energy. The weather was horrendous and the playing surface more like a cabbage patch.

IN PROFILE

CHRIS HONOR

After a run in the first team last season, Chris Honor's first team appearances have been limited this season to one League game at Northampton and a Littlewoods Cup match at Reading.

He is hoping that his month on loan at Fourth Division Hereford will help him in his bid to reclaim a first team place at Ashton Gate.

"I jumped at the chance of a loan spell as reserve games haven't been too frequent of late. Even so, I think it's fair to say that reserve team football lacks the competitive edge of League football and hopefully my month at Hereford will sharpen me up".

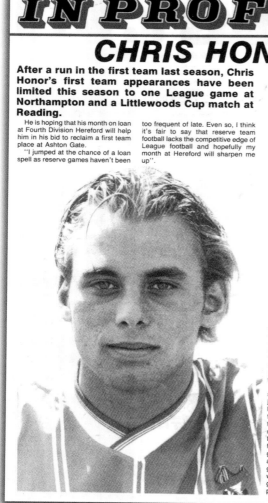

Chris made his first appearance for Hereford on New Year's Day against Gillingham and admits that he found it a little strange.

"I played at right back and the strangest thing was pulling on a white shirt. Things went reasonably well for me although the preparation for the game was completely different. I found the build up to the game was a little "laid back". Here at Ashton Gate, we've got used to our pitch warm up and the atmosphere is more intense to ensure that our attitude is right from the first whistle. In my first game there, no one knew the side until 2.15 and there seemed to be a lack of urgency".

His experiences at Hereford have helped Chris to appreciate what a club like City have to offer.

"I very much see Hereford as a "stop off" point. I don't honestly think I can progress there. If anything, I suppose I am in the "shop window" although I want to stay with Bristol City and still think I can do it here at Ashton Gate. They say the first season is the hardest in professional football and last season I got into the side and had a lengthy run. You feel the nerves inevitably and who will forget the big match atmosphere of the Nottingham Forest games. I felt I controlled my feelings and coped pretty well. Maybe on occasions, I was only doing just enough to get by. You apply yourself and try a bit harder, you know you have to".

Chris has slotted in at full back at Hereford, but with City he has played a fair amount of his football in midfield this season. Has he a preference?

"I don't mind where I play. At the start of the season, with Paul France joining the club, there was cover at full back and I was played in midfield. I felt capable of playing in a more forward, creative position. I was chosen to play in midfield against Manchester United in a pre-season friendly. It was a game where I feel I got found out. I do enjoy playing there and I have, I think developed my game going forward. I don't really know where I want to play, but for my own good, perhaps I've got to stick to one position in future".

Had the TV cameras not been present – and back then live games on television were rare – the match might even have been called off. I can remember tracking a run by Parker and moving in zig-zags because I knew where the pitch was softest. The ball would get caught up in the bog on occasions and by the end of extra time we were absolutely exhausted.

We had conceded a lot of possession to the obviously better team and just couldn't hold out in the closing minutes. Parker smashed one into the top left-hand corner of our net and it was a moment it took me years to get over. Older players like Steve Galliers were telling me to soak up the occasion because it didn't happen every season. But, while I still retain some happy memories of the day, the feeling I had at the end was probably the worst of any in my entire career. I was walking off the pitch in tears when Brian Clough came up and put his arm around me. I'll never forget him saying: "If you go on playing like that, son, you will play for England." Which just goes to prove he wasn't always right!

The following season brought promotion. It must have been a good time to be a City player.

We were growing with every season. From 1982 when the club almost went bankrupt there had been a gradual rebuilding process under Terry Cooper, then Joe Jordan, and it was great to feel a part of that. It came to fruition with promotion, although there was a sour taste to it in the end because Bristol Rovers pipped us to the Third Division title, something Geoff Twentyman never fails to remind me about when I work as a pundit for Radio Bristol. I was involved in only a dozen or so games that season, but still recall the mixed emotions at the end of it. I even received a message from a Rovers fan on the anniversary of our 3-0 defeat at Twerton Park in the penultimate game saying: "Thirty years on. How are you feeling?" I sent it on to Geoff, who texted back a smiley face!

You ended up leaving Ashton Gate in 1991 to join Scottish club Airdrie. How did that come about?

A good question. You shouldn't have regrets in life, but that decision is one I wish I could take again because the move turned sour in the end. I had fallen out of favour with Joe Jordan and after winning promotion only played in one game the following season. At the age 22, I thought I was better than that and became massively impatient, wanting to play every week. I looked at the players getting into the side ahead of me and, with a touch of arrogance, thought I was better than they were. So the following summer when assistant-manager Jimmy Lumsden said he had a friend up in Scotland, who was interested in taking me into the Premier League up there, I thought I would go, if only to show other clubs I was ready for a move.

I really enjoyed it and the attraction of playing at Celtic and Rangers persuaded me to sign a three-year contract with Airdrie. I was made to feel important at a relatively small club and I guess I was flattered. As it turned out, the whole time I was playing in Scotland I was having second thoughts. Terry Cooper, who was Exeter City manager at the time, had called me saying "Don't sign" because he was getting the Birmingham City job and wanted me to go there. He was my kind of manager and had brought me up at Ashton Gate, so I don't know what came over me when I did sign for Airdrie. Within a couple of days Terry rang again and I had to tell him what had happened. When he put the phone down, I thought "what have I done?"

It wasn't all bad because we achieved the highest League placing in Airdrie's history and got to a Scottish Cup final against Rangers at Hampden Park. I scored the winning penalty in the semi-final shoot-out against Joe Jordan's Hearts, which was more than slightly pleasing, although with hindsight there is no animosity over him deciding I was surplus to his plans at City. The following year I played in the European Cup Winners Cup with Airdrie against Sparta Prague and how many Bristol lads get to do that?

When you say the move turned sour, you are referring to the way it ended, which led to your being described as 'The English Bosman'.

It was in the days before freedom of movement like there is today. What Airdrie did was allowed my initial contract to run out and then offered me another one on less money, which I turned down. They then stopped paying my wages, but still refused to sell me. Gerry Francis took me to Queens Park Rangers, who were in the Premier League at the time, and there was an agreement with Airdrie that they would buy me for £70,000. From what I understood from the agent who was dealing with it, when push came to shove, Airdrie upped the asking price to £250,000, at which point Gerry pulled out.

By then I had spent six weeks at QPR, encountering many of my other old foes from Bristol Rovers in Ian Holloway, Gary Penrice and Devon White, and was basically there for

Chris in the press box at Ashton
Gate where he works regularly as
a pundit for BBC Radio Bristol

the whole of pre-season. I wasn't getting paid by Airdrie and I had a mortgage at the time, as well as a lot of other bills. Our union, the Professional Footballers Association, then approached me and said they would take my case to the European courts. I visited Brussels on several occasions and received good advice. After that I met the solicitor, who was working for Jean-Marc Bosman and it became a race to see which of our cases would go to court first. His got there about a month before mine and resulted in the 'Bosman Ruling', which led to players being free to move at the end of their contracts. The other way around and it might have been the 'Honor Ruling'.

I felt bitterly let down by Airdrie. They eventually gave me a free transfer, but a long period in my career had been wasted fighting my case and by then I had been out of the shop window for too long. Russell Osman, who by then was Bristol City manager, was kind enough to invite me back so I could keep my fitness levels up and the PFA were paying my wages. Then I put my foot down a hole on the training ground pitch, which had been used for a goalpost, and snapped my leg. It took about six months to come back from that and I was never really the same as a player from then on.

I was about to join Cardiff City when a consortium headed by Terry Yorath to take over the club fell apart and on the day I expected to sign a contract I had to leave. By then I realised my days as a player were numbered and I decided to get out of the game because I couldn't rely on it to give me a living anymore. On good advice, I bought a couple of Esso franchises, which meant I was based in Bath. After a little time with Bath City, Forest Green came in for me and I helped them win promotion to the Conference, while also playing at the old Wembley in the FA Trophy final. Looking back on my career as a whole, I feel I should have done a bit better and achieved more. But, despite the way my years as a full-time professional finished, I consider myself such a lucky guy, with a fantastic family and a great business.

LESLIE KEW

Les Kew was a new member of City's board when the club's financial problems reached crisis point in February 1982 and the only director to stay on when the new company, in which he invested, was formed. He served as vice-chairman under Des Williams and later became chairman.

How did you come to join the board of Bristol City?
There was a family connection. My uncle had been vice-chairman under Harry Dolman and Stephen Kew later served as a director prior to becoming chairman himself. Stephen was the adopted son of W.J. Kew, who served on the board and was my father's second cousin. A lot of people thought Stephen and I were brothers, but he was actually quite a distant relation, possibly my fourth cousin by adoption.

When I was a youngster, another uncle used to take me to Ashton Gate and I had to sit on someone's shoulders to get a clear view of the games. So I have been involved with City as a supporter pretty much all my life. Later, when I went into business, I was invited to join the 51 Club, which had been formed in 1951 by Harry Dolman, and was made up of professional people. Like any fan, I was a critic, as well as a supporter, and always felt things could be done better.

So, when the opportunity arose to join the board, I grabbed it. We had been through that wonderful period of the team playing in the First Division under Alan Dicks, but unfortunately things had collapsed somewhat following relegation and the club were in considerable trouble.

It was then that I bumped into Ken Sage, who also went on to be a director of Bristol City 1982 plc. We started discussing what was happening, what could happen and what might be done about it. Fortunately, we were able to put some things together and raise sufficient capital to help rescue the situation by means of some tough decisions and the formation of a new company. They were really difficult times, but exciting in a way and the action taken ensured there is still a Bristol City Football Club today.

Les takes centre stage at an Ashton Gate press conference, flanked by fellow directors Peter Manning (left), Oliver Newland (second left) and Ken Sage (far right).

You are unique in having been a director of the club before the dark days of February 1982 and also on the new board when it was formed.

That's quite right. I originally planned to invest in the club when joining the old board and a report appeared in the Evening Post, written by Peter Godsiff, to that effect. I had spoken to Peter, who became a very good friend, and at the time the story was correct. But I soon realised that, while I was keen to get involved, a number of the existing directors were looking to jump ship. I asked to see the accounts to assess the state of the finances and it became clear that any money I injected at that point would be swiftly swallowed up by what was owed in VAT or to the Exchequer.

It would have defeated the object, so I delayed investing and it was at the meeting I mentioned with Ken Sage that we decided to form a consortium to effectively close down the club and relaunch it as a new company.

It was always going to be difficult because the Football Association and Football League management committee were not happy with the plan. They were concerned with the welfare of the players and knew it would involve terminating contracts. That was not something we wanted to do, but we felt there was no other course of action if the club was to be saved. The consortium got together and raised sufficient money to take things out of the hands of the liquidators. But that was only part of the battle and unpopular decisions had to be made to carry through our rescue operation.

That takes us to February 3rd 1982 and the dramatic meeting at the Dragonara Hotel in Bristol. Eight senior players had been told they must either tear up their contracts or have no club to work for. How do you remember that day?

It is one that will stay with me forever. I was heavily involved, along with Deryn Coller and Ken Sage, who were also part of the rescue consortium, while the Professional Footballers' Association were also represented, supporting the players who came to be known as the 'Ashton Eight'. The most terrible thing about it was those players were my friends, lads I had followed, watched and almost worshipped at times as a supporter. Sometimes there are choices you have to make in life where you have to put personal emotions to one side. The objective was to save Bristol City Football Club and nothing could be allowed to get in the way of that.

I believe the players concerned understood that in the end. But it was extremely hard for them because they were sacrificing their careers. Most had wives and families to support and the wages they lived on were being

taken away from them. It was awful, but something we had to do. It reached a situation at the Dragonara where there was an impasse and agreement could not be reached between ourselves, the players and the PFA. At that point I clearly remember Ken Sage banging his fist on the table and saying "It is ten to twelve. If we don't come to a decision by 12 o'clock, I am walking away and taking my money with me." We had to have a deadline and that's how close it came to the rescue plan falling through.

Bristol City were ten minutes away from having played their last game. It was a case of either accepting the deal we had put on the table, or the club going out of business, because we had come up with every penny we possibly could. Thankfully, agreement was then reached and we were able to take things forward, but even then it was far from straightforward. Apart from the problems associated with launching the new company, we were, of course, desperately short of players.

The following Saturday a crowd of more than 9,000, nearly twice as many as for previous home games that season, watched a City team with four young debutants, battle out a goalless draw with Fulham at Ashton Gate.

Everyone was so relieved to still have a club to support and that was another unforgettable day. Our campaign slogan was 'Support Bristol City Now Or Never' and we even wore red

On the ball . . . Les practises his skills in Hyde Park prior to City playing at Wembley

and white hats that afternoon with 'Now Or Never' written on them. It was a huge attendance by our standards at the time and the youngsters (Rob Newman, Jon Economou, Wayne Bray and Mark Smith) played their hearts out under the guidance of Roy Hodgson, who had been appointed our temporary manager, having been assistant under Bob Houghton. All credit to Roy, who worked really hard with us during those difficult days and helped bridge the gap until we appointed Terry Cooper the following summer. The Fulham game was the start of a new era, but there were still many hurdles to overcome.

That season ended in relegation, as the previous two had done, and even worse was to follow as City dropped into the Fourth Division, actually propping up the entire Football League in 92nd place in December 1982. It was only then that the corner was turned.

Yes, even during Terry Cooper's early days as manager we were in dire trouble, but at the same time we never lost the enthusiasm over still having a club to support. There remained a belief that Bristol City would experience good times again and Terry was a huge factor in that. He actually approached me before he was appointed and said: "I'll come and I won't want any salary until we get things sorted. Then we can sit down and talk about a contract." So he worked for nothing to start with. How many managers today would do that? When we were at rock bottom of the League just before Christmas, he told me: "Don't worry. I've just signed a player, who is worth three." That was Forbes Phillipson-Masters!

Under Terry, the right atmosphere gradually developed at the club. He brought in Clive Middlemass as his righthand man and everyone worked so happily together. We were a team again, not just on the pitch, but in the boardroom and with the staff. Slowly we started to climb the table, the next season brought promotion and then came Wembley in 1986.

You are referring to the Freight Rover Trophy final win over Bolton Wanderers. Looking from the Royal Box at 30,000 City fans backing their team, how did you feel?

It's difficult to explain your innermost feelings, but of course I was emotional after all we had been through. It started the day before when we visited an empty Wembley for the players to train on the pitch, which was really exciting in itself. The directors were allowed onto the hallowed turf as well and we kicked a ball around like happy school kids. Did I ever think that would happen to someone who loved playing local football in my youth? Of course not, it was a dream come true. Then came the day itself, with the crowd, the colour and the atmosphere. To me, it felt like 100,000 people were there.

I remember the celebrations in the dressing room after the game and trying to avoid being dragged into the bath by the players. In those days, there weren't individual showers and all the lads jumped in together. Everyone was on a high and it was an unbelievable night. We remembered to look after the trophy, but what we forgot in all the excitement was that a brand-new minibus was part of the prize.

In the end, I was nominated to drive it back to Bristol, once we had all recovered from the celebrations a day or two later. Another director, Ivor Williams, came along for the ride and there were some other passengers. I remember thinking the engine was a bit sluggish as we made our way along the M4. It wasn't until we reached the M32 that I realised the bus had five gears and I had been driving all the way in fourth.

Great days and wonderful memories.

BRISTOL'S
SUBS BENCH

STEVE LANSDOWN CBE

Having been part of the consortium put together by Scott Davidson to take over Bristol City in 1996, Steve Lansdown succeeded John Laycock as chairman in 2002 and remained in the role for nine years. Since then he has been the club's owner and overseen the reconstruction of Ashton Gate, including the building of the Lansdown Stand, named in his honour, while also launching Bristol Sport to oversee the commercial running of City, Bristol Bears Rugby and Bristol Flyers Basketball, along with the City and Bears Women's teams.

Is it true that you followed Bristol Rovers before becoming a City supporter and shareholder?
Yes, I was brought up at Tockington in South Gloucestershire, north of the river, so my first football-watching was stood on the Tote End at Eastville. The reason I switched allegiance was that Rovers moved to play at Twerton Park in Bath and were not a Bristol side anymore. When my son Jon started to want to watch football, it made more sense to take him to Ashton Gate and that's how my involvement with City began.

When did sport first become an important part of your life?
I played both football and cricket at school and also later at local level. I played football first for Olveston United, who were the club nearest to Tockington, then for Almonsdsbury and in the Bristol and District League for Filton. It was pretty low-level stuff, but like most kids I always enjoyed kicking a ball around and dreamed of one day playing at Wembley. As far as cricket is concerned, I opened the batting at Thornbury Grammar School, although the teams I played in there were never that good.

When I left school I stopped playing cricket for a number of years, but took it up again when my son wanted to play and turned out for Bishopston Third XI for many seasons. The first year I topped the batting averages at the age of around 45! My interest in all sports was enhanced by television. As you watch those big moments when people cross the winning line to win a gold medal, or teams face each other in a major final, it makes the hairs on the back of your neck stand on end and you want to be part of it.

Given the chance, would you go to a football final at Wembley or a Test Match at Lord's?

It depends which football teams were involved. If Bristol City were one of them it would be a no-contest, but if it were a choice between watching maybe Chelsea face Tottenham Hotspur at Wembley or attending a Test Match, I would probably opt for the Test Match to be perfectly honest. I see a lot of football, so it's nice to spend time watching cricket.

You trained as an accountant. Is it true that Hargreaves Lansdown, the financial services company you helped build and which has made you among the richest men in the country was started in a bedroom?

Absolutely true. Peter Hargreaves and I met when we both joined a local brokering firm. Peter had come down from Lancashire and, while that job didn't work out for us, we talked about setting up on our own. As with all new businesses, it was necessary to keep costs under control. Peter had a mews cottage in Clifton and we started off running things from his front bedroom.

Things have moved on a fair way since then. Is it right to refer to you as a 'billionaire' and do you ever look in the mirror and think you haven't done too badly?

Technically yes, the term billionaire is correct. In this day and age you get the 'rich list' published in *The Sunday Times* and I find that a bit of an imposition. I feel somewhat embarrassed to talk about it, but it is a fact. As for looking in the mirror, it is not my way to think about what I have achieved. I am always thinking about what I can do next.

When did your involvement with Bristol City begin?

It was in the mid-1980s, when my son Jon was around six years old, that I first started taking him to Ashton Gate. But I was involved in a way before that because Des Williams, the former chairman, was one of my first clients at Hargreaves Lansdown. That is where the real connection stemmed from. We used to have lunch together and Des would tell me a few stories about what was going on in the background of the club, which I can now do myself with other people. I later became part of the consortium formed by Scott Davidson to take control of the club and joined the board as a result.

As owner of Bristol City, what has been your philosophy? Are you more of a Jack Walker or a Roman Abramovich?

I don't know either of those two gentlemen, so I can't really comment. As for my own philosophy, I remember listening on the radio many years ago to a Real Madrid match in Europe and hearing the noise of the crowd behind the commentary. At the time I thought wouldn't it be brilliant to have a team in Bristol doing that sort of thing and it acted as my inspiration. In the past I have been very hands-on as Bristol City owner, but since I moved to live in Guernsey I have left much of the work to other people. I want the community to be involved with the club and for the directors to know what is good, not just for the club, but for the fans. I want the players to think the same way and I think we are in a very good place as far as all of that is concerned.

What have been the highs and lows since you have been in charge of the club?

The highs are very simple, winning promotion in 2007 and then reaching the Championship Play-off final at Wembley the following year. Although we lost to Hull City, to get ourselves into a situation where we were one step away from the Premiership was a great achievement. There were 85,000 spectators at Wembley at the end of a memorable season and, while the game ended in heartbreak, the occasion will live with me forever. Probably the biggest disappointment was that we never kicked on from there and ultimately ended up getting relegated back to League One after six years in the Championship. That was the real low point.

You also suffered some major disappointments in efforts to see a new stadium built for Bristol City to play in. How demoralising was it when the Ashton Vale project, in particular, fell through?

It was a huge disappointment. The blow was really that, having put together a plan that I thought involved all parties on the council, it still ended up being thwarted. We are talking about a period of five to seven years battling to bring the plan to fruition. But that is all history and we are now looking at the redevelopment of Ashton Gate into a 27,000-seater stadium. It's all coming together and when you talk about high points, one is seeing those stands actually coming out of the ground and knowing they will help us to stage top-class football and rugby in Bristol at a top-class facility. I know seeing the old East End disappear was sad in a lot of people's eyes, but that was the start of the change. As a club, Bristol City are now looking forward, rather than backwards. We also invested heavily in a pitch, which is now first rate and will benefit both football and rugby players in the years ahead.

You mention Bristol Rugby. At what stage did you decide that they should be brought together with Bristol City?

There were many conversations over the course of the time I had been involved with City about the rugby club coming to play at Ashton Gate, but for one reason or another it never happened. What changed things was when Chris Booy (Bristol Rugby Club chairman) knocked on my door and asked me to put in some money because the club was going out

Steve may be a giant in the business world, but not when it comes to Bristol Bears Rugby as this photo with Steve Luatua proves

of business. Chris was a good friend of mine and I knew his passion for rugby. I wanted to support him, but even more importantly, I didn't want to see top class rugby disappear from Bristol. It could have happened. My words to Chris were that, whatever happens, we must have a professional rugby club in the city.

That was the starting point and it quickly became obvious that, if we were going to bring the clubs together, it made no sense for them to be playing at different grounds. Stadiums are very expensive to run, so you need as many people as possible passing through the turnstiles as often as possible. Having rugby as well as football played at Ashton Gate therefore made perfect sense. There were still a lot of people associated with the rugby who never thought it would happen and in the end I had to force the issue. I actually said: "this is when it is going to take place". If I hadn't done so, I think things would have drifted further and further backwards. Now the move has been made, we are seeing just how much passion there is for rugby in Bristol by the size of the attendances. It has worked out really well and all parties are happy.

Why did you set up Bristol Sport as a separate company?

The inspiration came from a visit to Barcelona's Nou Camp stadium and going into the museum there with all the trophies. I realised that Barcelona were also into other sports, such as basketball and water polo, among others, and it made me think what a good idea it would be for the same to apply in Bristol. To have Bristol City, Bristol Rugby, the Flyers basketball team, the women's football and rugby teams and other sports working off each other. It would help us promote sport in Bristol and make each of the individual clubs more successful. Bristol Sport was set up and has two main aims – to run all the commercial operations of the clubs concerned and to make sure the finances involved are being looked after in the right ways, working within budgets and avoiding over-spending unnecessarily, something I have to admit I had been guilty of in the past.

The people employed by Bristol City and Bristol Rugby focus on the playing side, getting the best players in and working towards the best possible performances on the pitch. Commercial matters and things like sponsorship are dealt with by Bristol Sport, along with the running of the stadiums. There is a discipline involved, which was missing before, and Bristol Sport is the hub of it.

Are you looking to bring more clubs or individuals under the Bristol Sport umbrella?

We are continually looking at all aspects. We receive many applications for financial help, but there has to be a commercial appeal, otherwise you are just giving money away. I am happy to invest in something if there is the chance of a return on that investment. We use the phrase to 'Inspire Sport' as our major goal because the more people who play or watch sport in the city, the better it is for Bristol sport in general.

Is Bristol really big enough to emulate Barcelona in sporting terms?

I have never compared the size of the two cities, but why not? Bristol is in a great position as the sixth largest city in England. It has a great catchment area and can support sport in a major way. There is a lot of passion for sport here, which just hasn't been given the opportunity to blossom. I believe that the sports I am not involved with, such as cricket, athletics and tennis, will feed off the success of the Bristol Sport companies. It is early days for what is a big project, but the signs are extremely encouraging. The degree of professionalism now in and around the Bristol Sports clubs pleases me no end.

ANDY LLEWELLYN

1982-1994

Having come through the apprentice ranks at Ashton Gate, Bristolian Andy Llewellyn made his League debut for City at Rochdale in December 1982 at the age of just 16 and went on to become one of the most consistent right-backs in the club's history, clocking up more than 350 appearances.

It's fair to say your first City appearance came with the club's fortunes at virtually rock bottom.

There was no money so we used to travel on the morning of away games, rather than overnight. The day before the Rochdale match, Terry Cooper told me I would be going there just for the trip and the experience of being with the squad. It was only when we were at the hotel where we stopped for lunch that he said I would be making my debut. That didn't give me much time to worry about it and I remember running out in front of a crowd of only around 1,300. We lost 1-0 and the defeat was a low point in the club's fortunes because it meant we were bottom of the entire Football League. The following week Terry played me again at Chester, where again we lost 1-0 in front of a small crowd, and after that he took me out of the team for a while.

In those days apprentices did unglamorous jobs around the ground such as cleaning the boots of the first team players. Were you still doing that when you got into the team?

Yes, even during the week leading up to the Rochdale game. We only had about 16 professionals at the time, along with five apprentices. It pulled everyone together and there was a great spirit about the club. If injuries were sustained, there was no money to go out and buy replacement players, so Terry and Clive Middlemass relied on lads from the youth team to bridge the gaps. That was great for us and we had some great senior pros to learn from in the likes of Tom Ritchie and John Shaw. Just training with them was fantastic and they helped the youngsters a lot. Terry himself was still playing and he was a huge factor in my career developing because every afternoon, after training in the morning and getting my apprentice jobs done, he used to take me out into the car park at

Andy battles for the ball with Bristol Rovers defender Vaughan Jones

Ashton Gate and have me clip balls to him. He had so much else to do because there were so few staff, yet he still took time to work with me individually and was massive in making me the player I became.

City's slide from the First Division to 92nd in the Football League finally bottomed out that winter. Did you feel the tide turning?

After what had happened to the 'Ashton Eight' and then hitting bottom of the Fourth Division, the only way was up. We had no set training ground and either used the car park or Ashton Park, but Terry always had faith that results would improve. He fostered such camaraderie among the players and staff, which proved key to gradually getting things right on the pitch. I remember Christmas 1982 as the first indication that better times were ahead. We lost at home to Port Vale on Boxing Day, but 24 hours later we had to visit Hereford United and found that Terry had pulled a masterstroke by bringing Chris Garland back to the club. The team coach picked him up at Chepstow racecourse on the way to Hereford and the moment he got on gave everyone a big lift. He was a hero to me and a legend with the fans. At the same time Terry brought club chaplain Derek Cleave to the club and he spoke to us for the first time in the dressing room before the match. We beat Hereford 3-1 and from then on our form improved. We finished mid-table and the worst times were behind us.

Promotion was achieved the following season and your City career also included three memorable FA Cup successes. What do you recall of the 3-1 fourth round win over Chelsea in January 1990?

Chelsea were one of the teams I supported as a schoolboy. I used to watch them a lot at the time of Peter Osgood, so just drawing them in the FA Cup was a thrill, particularly as cup draws had been pretty unexciting for us over a long period. The team we faced had players of the calibre of Graham Roberts and David Speedie, but it was a typical day for a shock result because the weather was wet and the pitch heavy. We were going well in the Third Division and fancied our chances. Bob Taylor was scoring goals for fun, but it was his strike partner Robbie Turner's day as he netted twice. Robbie still talks to this day about the match as his main claim to fame! I particularly remember the first goal because I got forward and put in a weak shot, which Dave Beasant only parried. Bob Taylor missed the ball as it bounced back and Robbie stuck it in. I have always claimed an assist! Mark Gavin got our other goal and we played really well. We had some exciting players at the time, with Gav and Dave Smith on the wings, and a set 4-4-2 formation, which suited us. Mark was the more tricky winger, but Dave had searing pace, which caused havoc for defenders. It was attacking side, with midfielders like Gary Shelton. On that day we played with flair and without fear. We thoroughly deserved to win.

A second FA Cup win fans remember with particular pride was the 2-1 fourth round win at Leicester City in January 1992, achieved on a frozen pitch thanks largely to a certain Jacki Dziekanowski.

On the morning of the game we weren't sure it would be played because there was a big freeze affecting most of the country. At the hotel where we had stayed overnight Jacki was my roommate. He had not long joined us and was great company. When the match was given the go-ahead we all switched on, but didn't realise until we got to the ground that it was to be covered by Match of the Day. So many games were off due to the weather that the cameras had been switched to Filbert Street. I can still hear John Motson's commentary where he said that Dziekanowski looked like he had come from a different planet. That's how good Jacki was on a treacherous pitch.

He was probably the most gifted footballer I played with during my time at City. Manager Jimmy Lumsden had known him from his Celtic days, but the rest of us didn't know what to expect when he signed. He proved a real character and as a player just when you thought he was having a quiet game he would do something outrageous with the ball to create a chance or score a goal. People used to say I did Jacki's running for him because he played in front of me a lot. My response was always: "Yes, but I can't do the things with the ball he can do." Some of the tricks he came up with in training were unbelievable. The cameras being present gave him the stage he loved and the atmosphere at Filbert Street was tremendous in those days.

Half the pitch was fine and the other half rock hard in places, but Jacki made it look easy to play on. He wasn't alone because Junior Bent had an exceptional game and actually managed to score for once! He was a lovely lad and we used to rib him about the number of chances he missed, but that afternoon he was electric and Leicester couldn't live with his pace.

Surely your greatest FA Cup memory of all must be the 1-0 third round replay win over Liverpool at Anfield in January 1994, a night that will live with City fans who made the trip forever.

Yes, when supporters talk about the FA Cup to me it is usually that game they want to discuss. Obviously, it was an unforgettable night and Brian Tinnion's goal is one of the most celebrated in City's history. We thought we had a good chance, having held Liverpool to draws in the home game at Ashton Gate, which was abandoned because the floodlights failed, and when that match was replayed. But when you consider the players in that Liverpool team it was still some achievement to beat them at Anfield. Unfortunately, there

Andy takes centre stage with team-mates on the Wembley pitch prior to the 1987 Freight Rover Trophy final against Mansfield Town. The author is taking the photograph

was a downside for me as I got booked on the night and lost my place in the team as a result. I played in the next game against Tranmere Rovers, but was then suspended and it proved my last appearance for City. So, while it's great to say that one of my final games was such a big one, there is a tinge of sadness about it too.

You were also part of the City squad for two Wembley finals in the Freight Rover Trophy, starting against Mansfield Town in 1987, having been an unused substitute against Bolton Wanderers a year earlier.

That competition to me summed up the highs and lows of professional football. While it was great to be going to Wembley with the lads in 1986, I was desperate to get onto the field. When we went 3-0 up I thought Terry was sure to put me on, but he got carried away with the emotion of the occasion in the closing stages of the game and by the time he remembered I had been warming up for quite a while the final whistle went. I was absolutely distraught. Leading up to the game there had been a few injury scares, including one with David Harle, and having gone on as a sub in the semi-final win over Hereford at Ashton Gate, I thought I would be next in line. Rob Newman would probably have been switched to midfield, with me taking over at right-back. But who is going to fail a fitness test with a Wembley appearance at stake? David recovered in time and the rest is history. We later found out that Mark Gavin was relieved to have Rob, rather than me, marking him on the afternoon – although Rob did almost kick him into the stand with one challenge! On the pitch after the game, Terry put an arm around me and said: "You are young enough and will get another chance." My reaction to that wasn't printable, but as

usual he turned out to be right and a year later I achieved my dream to play at Wembley. The Mansfield game went to a penalty shoot-out and eventually sudden death. Neither David Moyes nor I had taken one and we both looked at one another. He said: "I think you're next" and I replied: "No, you are." He went up and missed, so in a way it was my fault we lost! At the time it was bitterly disappointing, but I can always say I played at Wembley, which is something a great many top players never did.

Renowned for your tough tackling, there were occasions when it got you into trouble. West Ham manager Billy Bonds once described a sliding challenge that saw you sent off in a match against his team as a "next stop Barking job".

I remember that well because the lad I tackled, Stuart Slater, went on to play for Weston-super-Mare, where I live, at the end of his career. He took great satisfaction in showing me that he still had the scar from that night. It was on his thigh!

GEOFF MERRICK

1967-1982

Few players experienced more contrasting emotions in their City careers than Geoff Merrick. Among the highs was being the Bristol Boy who captained the team that won promotion to the top flight of English football in 1976 and led them out at Arsenal in the opening game of the following season. Contrast that with the devastating low of ending his career with the Robins as one of the Ashton Eight.

How did your association with City start?

I grew up only ten minutes away from Ashton Gate and used to walk to games carrying my boots when I first started playing. My mum and dad were both ardent City fans and my dad took me to games from the age of around seven. I played for Bristol Boys through the age groups to when I was 15, at which time I signed up to become a painter and decorator when I left school. I had played for England schoolboys, but although other clubs were interested in signing me, Bristol City left it very late to make contact. One night, about two weeks before I was to finish school, there was a knock on my door at home and it was Cliff Morgan, the club's scout, to say they wanted me at Ashton Gate.

When did you first get an idea that something special was building under Alan Dicks' management?

There were a few seasons leading up to promotion where we finished not too far off the top of the Second Division and it was obvious that we were gelling as a team. A lot of the players were young and had played in the youth team together and it was a case of giving us time to develop. We added a number of key signings from Scotland, such as Gerry Gow, Tom Ritchie, Gerry Sweeney and Donnie Gillies, and there was another one, Billy Menmuir, who never quite made it, but was another super player. He came down with Gerry Gow and they used to stay in a council house about five minutes' walk from my home.

Billy was probably a better all-round footballer than Gerry, but never had the same relish for getting stuck into opponents that Gowy had to go with his considerable ability. The Scotsmen blended in incredibly well with the six or seven Bristol lads in the squad and a lot of them became adopted Bristolians, who stayed living here when their playing careers

Ashton Gate's pin-up boy. The caption to this photo read: Geoff loves the outdoor life and spends his spare time down on the farm

ended. They never developed a West country accent though! I think without a shadow of a doubt that having so many local boys playing for City at the same time was an advantage because we all felt something special for the club. Take Trevor Tainton. He wore the red shirt for the best part of 20 years. These days players come from all over Europe and don't stay 20 minutes! For a Bristolian schoolboy, who was a City fan, playing for the club was the best thing you could do. That's where that extra passion comes from.

When I woke up in the morning, I used to think I had the best job in the world. To tell people I was going to work was kidding them. I used to start days at the Robin Café with a cup of tea and a piece of toast before we started training. The players would meet there before going down to the dressing rooms. We had fancied our chances the season before we went up and were in with a chance right up until a game at Leyton Orient late in the campaign when there was a problem with the floodlights. They had a little chap up front called Derek Possee, who I had played against many times because he was also at Millwall for some years, That night he did something a bit different, which came off, to score the only goal and I was angry with myself. When the lights went off it looked as though we might be reprieved, but it didn't happen and it was one of the worst trips home I ever had because I knew we had let a great opportunity slip away. Thankfully we only had to wait another year for the dream to be realised.

What are your memories of the amazing night of April 20th 1976 when the Bristol City team you captained beat Portsmouth 1-0 at Ashton Gate to clinch promotion to the First Division?

I remember most vividly the closing minutes of the game. We had scored early, but then not played well and it became a really nervy evening. My right-foot was for standing on and I sliced an attempted clearance wide of goalkeeper Ray Cashley almost into our own net. The closer it got to full time, the more supporters spilled over onto the touchlines. It got so tense that I actually tapped the referee on the shoulder and said: "If you don't finish this game soon, they score a goal and we don't get promoted, you are going to get murdered! So blow the whistle." He walked back a few paces, looked at his watch as they took a goal kick, and blew for full time. It was a fabulous night and I only wish I could go back over it again in slow motion. There wasn't the television coverage of the game there would be today, so we all have to rely on our memories. If I had film of the match, I would probably look at it once a month at least because it was such a wonderful experience. What pictures do exist show the crowd running onto the pitch at the end and there are some of me up in the directors' box for some reason looking really miserable. I don't think it had quite sunk in what we had achieved. People were in tears because they never thought that after 65 years they would ever see Bristol City back in the top flight of English football. I was in a daze, looking down on all the fans massed out on the pitch. I had done the same as them as a kid, leaping over a gate to get onto the field when the club won promotion from the Third Division in 1965, led by the great John Atyeo. I could picture Big John up in the same stand, alongside his team-mates, with both arms raised in triumph and I tried to give a similar salute.

We had a great side, not only full of really good players, but really good people too. We all got on well together on and off the pitch. For five or six years it was the perfect scenario in which to play football and achieve success. And we had a much closer relationship with the fans than is the case today. They were everywhere and we used to go for a pint with some of them in the Smyth Arms, as it was then called, in Long Ashton. After games we would go up into the Supporters Club. If we won, it would be drinks all round and if we lost there might be a bit of banter. We were always in the same places as the fans, whether it was the post office, the shops or the pubs. It was the same before I played. I was a Bedminster boy and I used to regularly see the stars from the City teams of that time. We just carried that on.

What about the celebrations that followed?

We still had our final game to play at home to Notts County the following Saturday. What happened between the matches is a blur, but we lost 2-1 and the celebrating probably had something to do with that. What I do recall clearly was the open top bus ride around Bristol. We went around some wonderful areas, including Hartclifffe and Knowle West, both with a massive City following, and ended up on College Green where I made a short speech, wearing a green suit. On the bus I had on this wonderful sheepskin coat with a seam down each side at the front and a massive collar. I think it finished up in the dog basket at home. It was the time of large-collared shirts and big ties. The bus ride was a brilliant occasion, but if it happened now and City reached the Premier League it would be ten times bigger. We didn't play our success down, but these days it would be feted even more.

It was reported that you came close to joining Arsenal during the promotion season. What was the story there?

Not so long ago I discovered some old scrapbooks and cuttings, one of which went as far as to say that the following week I would be an Arsenal player. They apparently wanted to sign myself and Tom Ritchie and the offer was around £240,000 for both of us. That was reasonable money back then, but nothing too dramatic. I did go to see Alan Dicks and the chairman Robert Hobbs to see what was happening. They made me a wonderful offer to stay, linking my wages to the retail price index, which meant that when nothing came of the Arsenal move, I finished up about 20 quid better off the following season! My wife would have loved going to London to live, but I was a town boy, who had developed a love of the countryside and I remember saying to her: "If I go to Arsenal, I might never see another cow". To be honest, I was quite relieved when the whole thing blew over. At the end of the season I took my father to Wembley to see the FA Cup final in which Southampton beat Manchester United. Who should I meet coming down the steps but the Arsenal manager, who I had met on holiday in Tunisia the year before and got friendly with.

He said to me: "Why didn't you come to us?", to which I replied: "Nobody ever told me the deal was on." Then he said: "You only had to pick up the phone and let us know you were keen." Can you imagine? Me, Geoff Merrick, of Bristol City, ringing Arsenal. I was honoured to even be linked with them. The fact was that I enjoyed playing for City so much that I couldn't really contemplate going anywhere else. I did have another offer later to go to Wolves, who were prepared to make me captain. By then I was on the fringe of City's team because Norman Hunter had been signed and I wasn't playing particularly well at left-back. The Wolves manager told me he would put me on the same money as John Richards, their star striker, and I thought about it really hard. But in the end I rang the club and turned down the move.

You and Gary Collier had developed a fantastic partnership in the centre of defence.

Yes, I probably played the best football of my life in the promotion season. I was voted Player-of-the-Year by the supporters during our four years in the First Division, but the last time it happened was the season we were relegated so it wasn't much to shout about.

Your biggest moment as a City player was surely leading the team out at Highbury for the opening game of the 1976-77 season against Arsenal. Can you remember your feelings in the tunnel?

We were all in a bit of a haze because it was almost too much to take in. It was certainly too much for chairman Stephen Kew, who when we were on the team coach approaching Highbury, turned to Brian Drysdale and me and said: "My God, we have got some support here today." I replied: "Stephen, Arsenal play in red and white." We actually played in a really great kit of white shirts and black shorts. I recall Brian particularly loved the black socks because he thought they made his legs look bigger! Arsenal had a raised pitch in those days. To be standing in the tunnel looking upwards into the sunshine and seeing just the heads of the supporters waiting for the teams to appear was unreal. All the things I had seen on TV over the years were about to happen to me.

I remember when we took the field that Highbury didn't look as big as I expected. After that everything went so quickly. I wouldn't say it was the best experience because I have more vivid memories of other big games. But to beat the Arsenal on their own patch wasn't a bad start to life in Division One. Clive Whitehead was absolutely brilliant. He was capable of doing so many things on the wing and that day he did it all. I was marking a chap called Malcolm MacDonald, who had arrived at Arsenal that summer for big money. At least, that is my story. Gary Collier always tells people he had 'Supermac' in his pocket, but I'm sure he was in mine! Whatever the case, he didn't get a kick.

Date: Saturday, August 21, 1976. Place: Highbury Stadium. Geoff Merrick leads Bristol City into the First Division after a break of 65 years. Gerry Sweeney follows his skipper on to the Arsenal turf

How big a blow was losing Paul Cheesley just a game after he had scored the winner in the opening First Division match at Arsenal?

Paul was becoming a great player when injury ended his career. How far he would have gone we will never know, but at the time what he was doing was making us a good team and there was so much more to come. He was still learning the game and what happened was tragic for him and the club because you couldn't replace him.

Tell us about some of the players you played against. In the Seventies every top club seemed to have exciting individual players.

How long have you got? There were some great players around. My favourite to play against was Kevin Keegan because his game suited me. I used to make him angry and he didn't like having me as an opponent. When he went to play in Germany he bumped into my brother, who was in the Army over there, and told him I was the best defender he had played against, which was quite a compliment. One striker I could never quite catch was Trevor Francis, then with Birmingham City. He was direct and loved running with the ball at pace. Another who always gave me trouble was Kenny Dalglish. A fantastic player. What would he be worth today? He would receive the ball inside the box with me behind him and it was just as though he was in the middle of the pitch because he seemed to feel no pressure. He would shield the ball so well and if you tried to get it and kicked him it would be a penalty. He had everything and was a nightmare for defenders. Back then every First Division team seemed to have at least three great players. Even the likes of Stoke City had top individuals and they were all British. There were some foreign imports, but it was a time in England where so many young boys aspired to be professional footballers. Where are they all now? Playing computer games when my generation would be off to Ashton Park for a kick-around.

The Bristol City side you played in beat all the top clubs in the country after winning promotion. And you even did the double of Manchester United when they were in the Second Division.

Yes, I remember the game at Old Trafford that season particularly upset their manager Tommy Docherty. My great friend Brian Drysdale was at left-back that day and he had a marvellous sense of humour, even when a match was in progress. United were giving us a chasing and we were defending like hell towards the end. In the space of about five minutes, Brian kicked two of their efforts off the line and headed another one out. When I looked at him he was almost creased up with laughter. He couldn't believe what he had just done. There were the two of us in our penalty area, with thousands of United fans baying for our blood, and we were in fits of giggles. That was typical of Brian. Everytime he did something really good, he would burst out laughing.

Even without Paul, you just about managed to stay up that first season in the top flight. How did you manage it?

I think it was simply that we were a pretty good team, with or without Paul. We still had great spirit and were never beaten because we gave up. Everyone kept on giving everything until the final whistle and, although a lot of people had written us off approaching the last games, we did enough to go to Coventry for the final match still in with a chance of staying in the First Division. No one expected us to beat Liverpool at Ashton Gate. Maybe their true team didn't turn up that night because they had bigger things on their minds, but it still took some effort to win 2-1 and keep our hopes of avoiding relegation alive. The famous draw at Coventry kept us up and over the course of the four years we were in Division One we beat all the top sides at one time or another. When I later became a builder, my colleagues would be fascinated to hear stories of what it was like to play at Old Trafford and Anfield or to chase after players like Francis and Dalglish. These days I do a lot of tractor driving as a farmer and during long days out in the fields memories like that often spring to mind. It was a great time.

Geoff fronts up to journalists reporting on the 'Ashton Eight' story. Behind him are David Rodgers and Chris Garland

We can't finish without touching on how your City career ended. What was it like to be one of the eight players told they had to sacrifice their contracts to keep the club in existence?

Apart from incidents that have happened within my family, of which there have been a few, it was the most tragic time of my life. Today if you stay in the Premier League for four seasons and get the parachute payments when you go down it is seen as success and a stepping-stone for kicking on again. With us, we had the four seasons and then everything went to pieces financially at the club. It wasn't as if millions had been spent to keep us in the First Division. Or if they were, I didn't see any of the money! We were on reasonable wages and no more than that. Given the opportunity, I would like to ask a few questions even now about what went wrong because we were getting good gates. Football was relatively cheap to run in those days and that applied to us as a team. None of the players were draining money out of the club. When I think back, I firmly believe what happened to the eight of us never should have happened. I am glad the club was saved, but the way it was done and the effect it had on the players concerned and their families was a disgrace. It was a terrible way for me to finish what had been a fantastic Bristol City career.

As you drive past Ashton Gate today, do you wish you had played at the stadium it has become?

To be honest, I wouldn't swap with what the City players have today. Even before the Dolman Stand was built, the ground had a fantastic feel about it. I loved every minute of those early days and wouldn't exchange my career with anyone. I only wish I could have it all over again.

SCOTT MURRAY

1997-2003 & 2004-2009

Scott Murray joined City midway through the 1997-98 season, which ended in promotion, and went on to make more than 350 League appearances in two spells with the Robins, as a winger or wing-back. He helped the club win the LDV Vans Trophy in 2003 and clinch promotion again in 2007, either side of a move to Reading, later taking up the role of kit-man at Ashton Gate.

You joined City from Aston Villa, but it might well have been Liverpool had a player who went on to become a close friend not unintentionally intervened.

Yes, I was playing in the Highland League in Scotland with Fraserburgh and was invited down for a couple of trial spells with Liverpool. The first week went really well and I remember meeting Scott Paterson, who later moved to City. I was then asked back to play in an actual game at Anfield. Big Ron Yeats, a Liverpool legend, met my dad, my brother and me off the plane and took us to the ground, which was empty for the reserve match I played in against Leicester City. We won 1-0 and I scored the goal at the Kop End. I remember celebrating as if the stadium was packed because Liverpool were the Premier League team I followed.

I was on cloud nine when I spoke to manager Graeme Souness after the game and everything was going according to plan. Back home I couldn't sleep, waiting for the phone call I was sure would come. It never did because shortly afterwards a certain Geordie lad called Brian Tinnion, with not a bad left foot, scored an FA Cup replay winner for Bristol City at Anfield and Souness was sacked. That was the end of my dream.

To this day I think Bruce Grobbelaar must have taken a bung to let Tins beat him. I was lucky enough to be Brian's best man at his wedding years later and I can assure you it got mentioned on the day that he owed me a few bob. I took revenge by putting extra alcohol in some of his drinks so that by the end of the day he couldn't stand up.

Despite that setback, you eventually moved into English football with Aston Villa. How did that come about?

I played well against Elgin City on a Saturday and their boss John Teasdale was good mates

with the assistant manager at Villa. He ended up driving me and another Fraserburgh player to Villa Park for a week and again I was invited back at the end of it. This time I scored a hat-trick inside 12 minutes, the fastest ever in a Premier League reserve match, and, with no Tins around to interfere, the manager Ron Atkinson decided to sign me. I remember going back home to my job at a fish market for a week to help out because they had been so good in giving me time off. Then it was back to Birmingham to start my career in England.

That was in 1994. Three years later you became a City player in the midst of a memorable season at Ashton Gate. What do you remember about that move?

Mainly that I knew nothing about it until it happened. I had played in a reserve game at Villa Park and Doug Ellis, the chairman, called me into his office. I got on really well with 'Deadly Doug', bless his soul, who was really good to me, but on this occasion he said simply: "Scotty, we've sold you". It turned out to be City who had come in for me and at the time I only knew where two places were, Aberdeen and Birmingham. So I asked Doug where Bristol was and when he said south my heart sank. I then drove down with my agent to look at the stadium, which was nothing like it is today, but still impressive, and I had checked that City were second in the league behind Watford, attracting decent crowds. As I was playing reserve team football in front of a man and his dog at the time, I was delighted to sign, particularly after talking to manager John Ward, who really sold the club to me.

Five months later you were celebrating promotion. That period must have been hugely enjoyable.

John Ward told me I would be in the team on the Saturday after I signed and then made me sub, so I knew straight away he couldn't be trusted! Only joking. John was an absolute gentleman and one of the nicest guys imaginable. I had joined Villa as a striker, but after Big Ron was sacked Brian Little started employing me as a wing-back because I had plenty of energy. It's known as the 'graveyard shift' because you are forever running backwards and forwards, but I knew City had signed me to play wide and was happy with that. I probably missed too many chances to make it as a striker, but I enjoyed working hard and managed to get my fair share of goals from the wing. In those days I could run the 100 metres in around 11.5 seconds, which wasn't bad for a small, skinny lad. I later watched Ivan Sproule when he joined City and I have never seen a faster footballer in my life.

We had a great coach in Terry Connor, who is another lovely bloke and whose coaching ability is second to none, and a great set of lads. Colin Cramb was a complete head case, so I tried to stay away from him as much as possible. Twenty odd years later I am still trying to avoid him! Shaun Goater was banging in the goals for us and we had a good sprinkling of local lads in the likes of Louis Carey, Tommy Doherty and Matt Hewlett. We really were all best mates. After training we would change in the old home dressing room at Ashton Gate and head off to Denny's in North Street to get a snack, a packet of crisps and a can of juice, to take back to the changing rooms. Then, having told wives or partners that we were doing a double session, we just sat there chatting and enjoying each other's company. With things going so well on the pitch, it was a very happy time.

Less than three months into the following season came the bombshell that saw John Ward depart following the club's decision to put Benny Lennartsson in charge. What do you remember of that time?

We played Bolton Wanderers on a Friday night and beat them 2-1 at Ashton Gate so we were in quite high spirits after a tough start to the season. The following Monday I saw John Ward walk onto the training ground looking as though he was carrying the weight of the world on his shoulders. Later we found out that Benny Lennartsson had been brought in and it was a shock to all of us. The board had obviously decided to take a new direction and, while they were fully entitled to do that, it certainly backfired. Benny didn't speak much English, a bit like myself! So it was hard for him to get his ideas across.

He actually ended up having a really good career, but the players felt hugely disappointed because we considered ourselves one big family under John and that family was torn apart.

The club had spent a lot of money the previous summer, bringing in the likes of Ade Akinbiyi, Tony Thorpe and Soren Andersen, so perhaps the chairman expected instant success at the higher level. Not so long ago Fulham splashed out big money on getting

to the Premier League, only to get relegated straight away. I think a better policy is to keep faith with the lads who have won promotion, at least until Christmas, and let them have first go at building on what they have achieved. In our case, it was a big step up and we took time to adjust, but the win over Bolton saw us climb the table and there was a feeling in the dressing room that we were starting to adjust. We tried to get on with things after John left, but ended up bottom of the table.

Let's skip a couple of seasons and move on to Danny Wilson's spell as manager, which so nearly brought promotion, and included a trophy win.

The years I played under Danny were great for me personally. He was undoubtedly one of the best managers I worked with, having been forward thinking as a player and adopting the same approach to being in charge. He kept things simple, telling defenders to defend and attackers to be really positive. Getting to the LDV Vans final at the Millennium Stadium in 2003 was a highlight in my career and to end up winning 2-0 against Carlisle United in front of around 40,000 City fans, who had travelled across the Severn Bridge, was a brilliant experience.

We were playing a team from a league below us, so the pressure was on our shoulders. But on the day we completely dominated the game and were worthy winners through goals from Lee Peacock and Liam Rosenior. For any lower league player to appear in a big final is so special and it was like the FA Cup final for me. I had also been lucky enough to play for City at the old Wembley Stadium, when we lost to Stoke in the same competition, and despite the result that is still right up there with my best memories.

I recall watching the first game of our run to the Millennium Stadium and feeling devastated that I wasn't picked because I wanted to play in every game. We managed to beat Queens Park Rangers on penalties and no one got particularly excited. But as the final got closer it was a different story and that day in Cardiff will stay with me forever. I can still picture Tommy Doherty, another character and the driving force of our midfield, lifting the trophy. We had a pretty good night!

The following season brought a Play-off Final against Brighton, which ended in defeat and another change of manager.

That was a really bad day for us. The only goal came so late in the game that we had barely any time to recover. Leon Knight converted a penalty conceded by Danny Coles and Brighton put ten men behind the ball in the final few minutes to protect their lead. We felt that we should have gone up automatically that season, so to lose to them was a huge disappointment. I would rather have finished seventh than get beaten in the Play-off final. It was shattering.

I was away on holiday the following week when I got a phone call saying Danny Wilson had been sacked. It is always sad when that happens and I was especially upset because I felt I had my best years as a player with him in charge. But as a professional footballer you soon have to switch your focus onto getting into the team under the new manager – and he turned out to be my old mate Tins.

You were in your second spell with City by then, having returned from Reading. It brought another promotion success under Gary Johnson before your career ended, but there was to be a third stint in a very different role.

I finished up playing non-League football, first for Yeovil and then at Bath City where I had two very enjoyable seasons. Towards the end of the second, I was also doing some coaching for Bristol City's Academy and one day I was driving when the name of Derek McInnes,

then manager at Ashton Gate, came up on my phone. I thought I must have done something wrong, but when I called him back he said he just wanted to give me a heads-up that the kit manager was leaving at the end of the season. He thought I would make an ideal replacement because I was a bubbly lad, who knew and got on with everyone at the club, and said the job was mine if I wanted it. I asked for 24 hours to think it over, but it was a no-brainer really. By that time I was around 37-years-old and it was taking me a fortnight to recover each time I played a game. Deep down I knew my playing days were over and that the job being offered was one I could do for the next 20 years or more.

I had been working in the commercial department at Ashton Gate while playing for Bath, so I had never really left. Being a kit-man is a bit like being a goalkeeper. You need to be a bit loopy! So I thought I fitted the bill. It has kept me involved in and around the dressing room and, while it was a lot to learn to start with, I have loved every minute of it. On the pitch I was a grafter and it doesn't worry me a bit that it is not a glamorous job. I have two lovely laundry ladies, who do most of the washing, and if for some reason they can't come in, I can do it myself.

It's long hours, but I get to watch games from the tunnel at Ashton Gate or the dug-out at away games, which is great. I have my own little kit bag carrying things like a spare pair of shorts and socks, a cap for the goalkeeper, studs, shin pads and anything that might need replacing during a game. After so many years, I am just pleased to still be involved.

BRISTOL'S
SUBS BENCH

STEVE NEVILLE

1984-1987

After starting his career at Southampton, Steve Neville played for Sheffield United and had two of his three spells with Exeter City before moving to Ashton Gate in the autumn of 1984. He was Bristol City's top scorer with 25 goals in the 1985-86 season, which ended with him being named man-of-the-match in the Freight Rover Trophy final at Wembley.

You played for City mainly under Terry Cooper and a bit under Joe Jordan. How do you reflect on that time all these years later?

It was around November 1984 that me and my close friend Trevor Morgan were involved in a swap deal that saw him move to Exeter, while I signed for City. It became the most enjoyable spell of my career. We had a lot of quality in our squad and played really attractive football. It was a joy to be in the team and it was probably my most consistent period in terms of form. We never quite managed to win promotion, but winning at Wembley was very special indeed.

You later played for Terry Cooper again at Exeter. What did you like about having him as boss?

He just had that charisma about him. Players wanted to play for him and he was very astute tactically. Add that as a motivator he was second to none and you have one fantastic manager. Once you have spoken with him, how can you not like him and how can you not play for him? The main reason I left Bristol City to go back to Exeter was that Terry had taken over there. He offered me an assistant-manager's role and we ended up winning the Fourth Division title by a considerable margin. I played under quite a few different managers during my career and he was without doubt the best.

I was never quite sure how highly Joe Jordan rated me. I suffered a hamstring pull at Sunderland in the 1987-88 season, during which he took over from Terry and we reached the Third Division play-offs. I thought it was quite a bad injury, but Joe begged me to keep playing. I agreed to get by with injections and played in the remaining games, which ended with defeat by Walsall in the Play-off final. That made me feel I was wanted, but

Steve on the ball at Wembley in the 1986 Freight Rover Trophy final against Bolton Wanderers

my contract was up and Joe called me into his office, basically offering me nothing, but saying "take it or leave it". Typically, Terry was sniffing around to see what was happening and I jumped at the chance to play for someone I would run through a brick wall for.

Before we talk about the Freight Rover final of 1986, we must mention the semi-final against Hereford United. The second leg at Ashton Gate proved a massive night for you.

I'll never forget it as long as I live. We had lost the first leg 2-0 at Edgar Street and were absolutely devastated in the dressing room afterwards. Terry was furious. He walked in and said "Oh well, that's your chance of Wembley blown" and walked out again, slamming the door. He knew exactly what he was doing and it was an example of the way he could motivate us. To a man, we were all determined to prove him wrong.

On the following Friday night at Ashton Gate we took a while to get going and were still two goals down on aggregate at half time. But once Glyn Riley put us ahead on the night and Howard Pritchard's deflected effort levelled things the momentum was with us. Even so, the tie went to extra time and for me to net the winner with only a minute to go was unbelievable. To this day I don't know how I had the composure to delay my shot when Bobby Hutchinson headed the ball into my path and make sure of finding the bottom corner of the net. I did a sort of shimmy before striking the ball and where that came from I will never work out. Time seemed to stand still and a lot of supporters told me after the game that they thought I was never going to shoot. It was almost as though we had won the trophy because the big prize was getting to Wembley for the first time in the club's history and the celebrations were amazing.

By the time the final arrived, however, it was all about winning. And you did that in some style with a resounding 3-0 victory over Bolton Wanderers.
They actually started the game well and we were under pressure. Winger Mark Gavin, who later played for City, gave Rob Newman a tough time and their two strikers, Tony Caldwell and George Oghani, were causing us problems. They had a lot of quality and experience in their squad, with the likes of Phil Neal and Asa Hartford starting the game and big Sam Allardyce on the bench. The first goal was always going to be important and when Glyn Riley scored it not long before the interval it settled us down. In the second half we came out and played the sort of football we were capable of producing at our best. From back to front in our team we had players with a high level of ability and the two goals we scored reflected that.

You were named man-of-the-match, but would you have preferred to have been among the scorers?
I would love to have netted at Wembley. But the main thing was for the team to win the trophy and to play well myself to contribute to that was very satisfying. These days I would have been credited with a couple of assists and to set up the third goal, which was as good as you will see at Wembley, was particularly memorable. Brian Williams got the ball at left-back and fed Alan Walsh, who spread the play to Howard Pritchard on the

opposite flank. Pritch played an even better long diagonal ball back across the pitch to me and I cut inside to chip a cross onto Glyn Riley's head for his second goal. Then came the priceless moment of him leaping the advertising boards and landing with legs stretched out, only to be paralysed by cramp. He literally couldn't move. That was Glyn, flamboyant and relishing the big stage.

What were the celebrations like after the game?
It was quite muted when we first got back to the dressing rooms because everything felt a bit surreal. We just sat there trying to take in what we had just done. No one was going mad. We were

almost pinching ourselves to realise we really had just won 3-0 at Wembley. Of course, we were buoyant and when the drinks started to arrive the high spirits took over. We then went up to the room at the stadium set aside for our families before going back to our hotel for a meal. They tried to shut the bar early, but by then we were buzzing and the boys, especially Bobby Hutchinson, were having none of that.

It was a great night and the one thing I regret to this day is that I didn't know there was going to be an open-top bus trip around Bristol on the Monday. Being from London, I stayed at my mum and dad's house over the rest of the Bank Holiday weekend and missed it. I would have loved to be on the top deck of that bus going around the city and sharing our success with the supporters. Their backing at Wembley was so important to us and when I see pictures of the bus tour I feel so envious of the other players.

You emigrated to Australia more than 20 years ago. What were the reasons behind that decision?

It was really down to my wife Wendy, who was born in Australia. Trevor Morgan had gone to work there about a year before we moved over and he contacted me to say he knew of a coaching job that might suit me in Perth. Because Wendy had an Australian passport, it made it easier for us to make the change and she and our children were desperate to do so. I wasn't so keen because I am an Englishman through and through. But after some hesitation I agreed to giving it a try and as soon as I saw what Australia had to offer, in terms of lifestyle and sporting opportunities for my kids, all doubts were erased.

I joined Western Australia State League club Sorento as a coach and went on to become Technical Director, a post I held until recently, while also coaching the first team. Since entering my mid-sixties, I have taken a backward step in terms of giving up the TD role and just concentrating on working with the senior players.

What level do Sorrento play at?

It is only one level below the A League, in which Perth Glory are the local team, but there is a big gap because their players are full-time, while we only train two or three times a week. We have had players, including my son Scott, go on to play for A League clubs. He joined Perth Glory at the age of 17, having started with Sorrento, and his career as a right-back developed from there. Soccer (if you call it football over here the people think you are talking about Aussie Rules) is growing all the time. The national team have had periods of success, with a golden era not so long ago involving Harry Kewell, Mark Viduka, Mark Schwarzer and others. And the pathway for young players to make their way in the game is much clearer than when I first came over.

Do you still keep tabs on events at Ashton Gate?

Yes, Bristol City's is the first result I look for every weekend, even before checking how Exeter got on. There are lots of Bristol people living over here and I bump into them regularly. I have been to cider dos and Wurzel parties where I have actually been approached by City fans who were at Wembley in 1986. They still enjoy talking about the Bolton game and I love hearing that Bristol accent again. My daughter Danielle was born there and it brings back so many happy memories.

  I do miss England at times. I've been back on a few occasions, twice at Christmas because you can't beat that time of year over there. But a barbecue isn't a bad way of celebrating! I love being in Western Australia and we have made many good friends since coming over, most of them football people, who enjoy the beach or a day at the races. It's not a bad life.

BRISTOL'S
SUBS BENCH

GARY OWERS

Gary Owers joined City in December 1994, valued at £300,000 in the £750,000 part-exchange deal that took Martin Scott to Sunderland. He played in midfield and at full-back during his time at Ashton Gate, was an ever-present in the 1996-97 campaign and a member of the squad which clinched promotion from the Second Division the following season.

Let's talk about the promotion season under John Ward. You must have gone into it in confident mood, having reached the play-offs the previous season.

Yes, we had been beaten by Brentford over two legs in the play-off semi-finals, which was a disappointment at the time because we had gone into the games as the team in form. A lot of people fancied us to go all the way. Although I managed to score in the first leg at Ash-

ton Gate, we ended up being beaten convincingly (4-2 on aggregate). But there had been a buzz around the dressing room over the way we finished the regular season and we were able to sustain that through the summer.

You were captain at the start of the promotion campaign and it got off to a dramatic start away to Grimsby Town with a frightening injury to the club's latest signing.

I can still see that incident in my mind's eye. I think it followed a throw-in. Steve Torpey, who was known as a tough target-man, put everything into trying to flick the ball on and took the full impact of their centre-back's head as he came from behind to challenge. Steve, who had scored earlier in the game, was knocked clean out and it was one of the worst injuries of its kind I have seen. The whole ground went quiet and there was a lot of concern for him. When he regained consciousness, he couldn't remember his goal. It took him a few weeks to recover, but thankfully he was okay in the end.

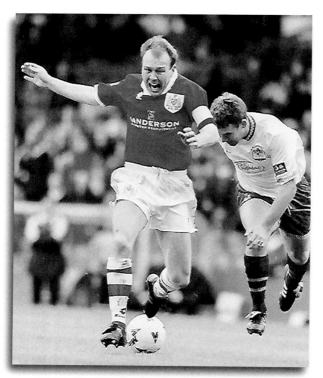

It didn't prove the best of starts to the season. Do you remember the angry crowd reaction when you drew at home to Bournemouth in the seventh League game?

It was a poor performance. Bournemouth were a young team at the time and I think Eddie Howe was playing for them. Everyone had expected us to make a flying start in the League, but it didn't happen and nothing went right for us that afternoon. We were slow off the blocks, only managed to draw 1-1, and the supporters let us know how they felt about us. You remember games like that and I had a few during my career. We were struggling to score goals, nothing was clicking and there was no fluency to our play. History shows that the team recovered and not long afterwards went on a tremendous winning run. Most of it coincided with me being out of the side, so we now know what the problem was!

You picked up a particularly nasty injury that caused you to miss 16 games. Tell us about that.

We won 2-0 away at Southend United, where I played in midfield with young Tommy Doherty, who was excellent on the day. Somehow I got a small sliver of aluminium stud lodged between two toes. Between the end of the game and a home match with York City the following Friday night my foot began to swell up, but the reaction seemed to be under control and I got through the York game, which we won 2-1. The next day I was in intense pain and when I kept looking at my foot it was getting bigger and bigger all the time. Once it got to about twice the size it should have been and felt like it was going to explode I rang our physio Buster Footman, who told me to get down to see him immediately and then made sure I went straight to hospital where I spent the next two weeks.

I came close to losing my foot through something like septicaemia and even today I feel really fortunate that it didn't happen. I don't think I was missed because when I did return to the ground it was two weeks before John Ward came to see me. "I didn't know you were back," he said. That may have been because by then the team were on a winning run of nine games and firmly on course for promotion.

Was it right that you nearly left the club at that stage?

The lads were doing so well without me. Tommy Doc and Matt Hewlett had come to the fore, while Rob Edwards had also played some games in midfield. Chris Waddle was manager at Burnley and made an inquiry. He was a friend of mine so I knew exactly what was going on. I went in to see John Ward, who was very forthright and told me: "I know you want to be playing, but I am going to be a bit selfish and whether you like it or not you are staying here." He added that he might need my experience to clinch promotion if things got a bit sticky at the end of the season and that's how it turned out. After the winning sequence ended, there was another team doing well in Watford and, while we didn't exactly stagger over the finishing line, we ended as runners-up when we should really have won the title. I got back into the side with eight games to go, which was great as I could share in all the celebrations. But looking back on my conversations with the manager it was clear he thought that Tommy and Matt were the way forward in midfield.

Who were the other key members of the team that season?

A fresh-faced Louis Carey, with no beard and his own fashion sense, played much of the season in central defence alongside a very good teacher in Shaun Taylor. I'm sure Louis would say that was a very important part of his education and I remember talking to him and Tommy Doherty in the dressing room after the disappointment of losing our final game at Preston North End, telling them to cheer up and enjoy the moment because promotion does not come along many times in a player's career. I was lucky enough at Sunderland to win a league in my first season and you can be fooled into thinking it will be success all the way.

Promotion is always a squad effort and it isn't fair to single out individuals, but we had a particularly strong left side, with Mickey Bell and Brian Tinnion. Keith Welch was a

really solid goalkeeper and we had very consistent performers in the likes of Rob Edwards, along with the wing skills of Greg Goodridge, plus a striker in Shaun Goater, who was always likely to grab a goal. Unfortunately, he was out of contract at the end of the season, so when the chance came for the club to get some money for him he was sold to Manchester City. The rest is history as far as his great career developed and thankfully we still had enough to go up following his departure in March.

Colin Cramb got a couple of goals in the game after Shaun left away at Wycombe Wanderers, which was a big result for us.

'Crammy' was a great character and I remember on the way to our opening game of the season at Grimsby when he was still new to the club he shouted down the bus "Hey, Owers, I hear your nickname is The Judge because you spend so much time on the bench."

When we got to the ground and John Ward named the team Colin found he was sub. He later came on for Steve Torpey, but was replaced before the end of the game. On the way back I said to him: "What was all that about me being The Judge? You are the first substitute I have ever seen substituted on his debut!"

One signing that didn't work out for John Ward was Sean Dyche, who went on to become a successful manager.

No, Sean came in and soon showed himself to be a very strong personality, having been part of a successful Chesterfield side, who had almost reached the FA Cup final the previous season. Unfortunately, he picked up a back injury early on and struggled from then on. When he did get into the team, he didn't have the best of times, which he would be the first to admit. But I am sure that now, with a few million in the bank as a top manager, he has got over it.

Watford, managed by John Ward's good friend Graham Taylor, ended up as champions. Both games against them were drawn, but the one at Ashton Gate is remembered for the state of the playing surface.

Our pitch was always lovely and green. I remember walking out of the tunnel that day and wondering what on earth had been done to it. Someone had the bright idea of staging a game of American football at Ashton Gate a couple of days before the two top teams in the Second Division faced each other and the line markings hadn't been removed properly. It was really confusing and you didn't know where you were on the pitch. The match was televised and the pictures didn't reflect well on the club. I didn't score many touchdowns in my career, but I think I got at least one, while also making a few tackles like the ones you see in American Football!

You scored in the final home game against Walsall, with promotion already guaranteed, and the match ended in scenes of celebration at Ashton Gate. What do you remember of that day?

I recall giving the ball away with my first three touches and getting a bit of stick from the crowd. Then Brian Tinnion swung a ball over from the left to the far post and I steamed in to head it into the net. It was a really nice moment and Brian scored from a free kick, which meant we won the game and could enjoy celebrating with the fans. But while that was going on someone decided to unfurl a huge banner proclaiming us Division Two Champions.

I don't know whose idea it was or where it came from, but it was embarrassing because we hadn't clinched the title. It came back to haunt us a week later when we lost at Preston and Watford overtook us. The banner was never seen again.

It was still a great season and all credit to John Ward, coach Terry Connor and the inimitable Buster Footman.

Absolutely. I have always respected John as one of the most natural coaches I have ever worked with. He had complete belief in what he was doing and I learned a lot from him. But as I later found out to my cost he also had a ruthless streak and wasn't scared to use it to benefit himself and his team.

Terry had been a very good player and was just making his way as a coach. He and John were a good team, very enthusiastic, and TC went on to have a very successful career as a coach at club and international level. Buster was a great character, wearing his tee-shirt in all weathers, and always telling us stories of his time in the Royal Marines. He and Junior Bent were forever having a go at one another. Junior used to say the only thing Buster did in the Army was peel the spuds, which didn't go down too well.

But it was part of some great dressing room banter and Buster got his own back by playing a tape of marching band music in the dressing room. If he wasn't out marching himself, he would be abseiling down some building on behalf of charity. Junior used to call him The Stunt Man.

GORDON PARR

1957-1971

Tough-tackling local product Gordon Parr was a member of City's 1964-65 promotion squad under Fred Ford, having signed for the club in February 1957. He made more than 300 appearances for the Robins during 15 years of service before ending his career in Ireland with Waterford.

How and when did your City career start?

As a Knowle West lad, I captained Bristol Boys, playing at centre-half, and had trials for the England Schoolboys team, which didn't come to anything. Bobby Jones, who later played for Rovers was in the same Bristol Boys squad. I had the chance to go to Wolves as a youngster, but the Midlands seemed so far away in those days because so few people had cars and I knew Bristol City wanted me. My parents insisted that I got a trade behind me because they didn't want me to end up with nothing to fall back on if football didn't work out for me. So I told the club I would sign if they could find me a job.

What was the response to that request?

The chairman of Bristol City at the time, Harry Dolman, offered me a job as an apprentice electrician at Brecknell, Dolman and Rogers, which was partly his company. I was 16 at the time and spent a few years combining that with my football. It proved good advice from my mother and father because, although I had a long career in the game, in later life I went back to working as an electrician. Pat Beasley was City manager when I signed. He was a quiet and somewhat moody guy as I recall, but I am not running him down because he was nice chap overall.

You were classed as a wing-half to start with and there are supporters today who wouldn't know what that position was.

It was the days of two full-backs, a centre-half and two wing-halves, with five attacking players in front of us. I might be classed as a midfield player in the modern game, but my main role was always to defend. It was my job to stop the people who could play in the opposition team from being effective. I liked a tackle, but one of my main assets was that

125

I could run all day. That came naturally to me, but I used to train a lot as a boy, going out running purely for the enjoyment.

After Pat Beasley, you went on to work with two other City managers in Fred Ford and Alan Dicks. What are your memories of them?

Fred and Alan were very different people, with very different styles of management. When Alan joined us, having been assistant at Coventry City a lot of things changed from when Fred was manager. I had my ups and down with Fred, who was old school, and one of our disagreements even ended up with us having a fight.

I had gone in to see him because he had dropped me and I wasn't happy because the team were not doing well. I asked what I had to do to get back in the side and his answer was that Chuck Drury and Jack Connor were both playing well, so he saw no reason for change. Then he added that he would never drop Gordon Lowe, no matter how badly he played. At that I lost my head and Fred's response was "I'll give you one minute, in which we will have a fight and sort things out." So we had a proper fight, but after a minute or so Fred said: "That's long enough. Let's go and have a drink." We did and that was that. It was a story of its time, all rather stupid and not the sort of thing that would happen at professional clubs today.

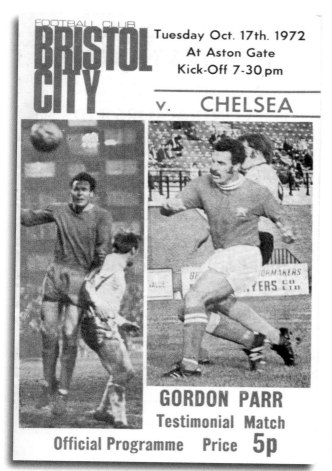

Who are the team-mates you remember most fondly from the 1964-65 Third Division promotion team and beyond?

Alec Briggs, who played at left-back, was a great mate and we have stayed friends to this day. We met as 15-year-olds and progressed up through the ranks at Ashton Gate together. The player I was usually closest to on the pitch was Jack Connor. Believe it or not, he was a centre-forward when he first came down from Huddersfield Town in 1960 and in that position he was absolutely hopeless. We all wondered why he had been signed, but when he moved back to centre-half he was brilliant. For year after year he was a really good defender, although he still thought he was a centre-forward at times! He was certainly no John Atyeo, who was the best player I ever played with. John was a top man and a great

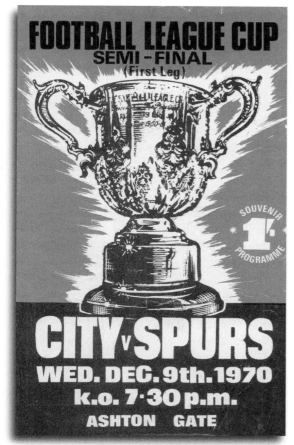

character off the pitch. He had come from the countryside and would say: "Alright my lover?" when he met you. He was a part-timer, like myself when I started, so it's amazing that he went on to play for England. Later I watched Chris Garland develop through the youth side and I played with him in the first team. He was always a bright talent and ended up moving to Chelsea while I was still at Ashton Gate. When my City career was coming to an end, I was awarded a testimonial and Chris organised it for Chelsea to come down and play us. It was brilliant for me to get a really top team from the First Division and I owe Chris a lot for that.

Apart from winning promotion with City, you played in a League Cup semi-final against Tottenham Hotspur in 1971.
We drew the first leg 1-1 at Ashton Gate, which was a great night. Spurs had some top players and Alan Gilzean got their goal, but we gave a good account of ourselves (Alan Skirton equalised) and it was wonderful to play in front of a 30,000 Ashton Gate crowd. If my memory serves me well, I believe we outplayed them in the second leg at White Hart Lane and had about six or seven chances to score. I won't name the player who missed most of them! They had only a couple of clear opportunities on the night and scored from both of them (Martin Chivers and Jimmy Pearce got the goals). We took the game to extra time and felt a bit hard done by to lose in the end.

Personality of the week

Birthplace
Bristol

Previous clubs
None

Signed
February 1957

Debut
at Leyton Orient,
January 11th 1958

Countries played in
Germany, France,
Holland, Spain

Most memorable match
at Tottenham in the F.A.
Cup 1967

Trade
Electrician

Ambition
To be successful in his
career when his football
days are over

Wife's name
Sheila

Other sport
Squash

Appearances
317

No. 1 — Gordon Parr

9

You had a glorious Indian Summer to your career after finishing at Ashton Gate thanks to an unlikely move to Ireland.
Games used to be played on a Sunday in Ireland so when I signed for Waterford I used to fly over on a Saturday and return home the following Monday morning. Shay Brennan, the former Manchester United full-back, was manager and he was a lovely man. We weren't a great side, but we were the best in Southern Ireland and I loved every minute of my time over there.

And you can actually say that you played in the European Cup.
That's right. We faced a club from Cyprus, Omonia, in the first round of the 1972-73 European Cup and I played in both legs. We won the home game 2-1, but then lost 2-0 over there in Nicosia. It was something I never

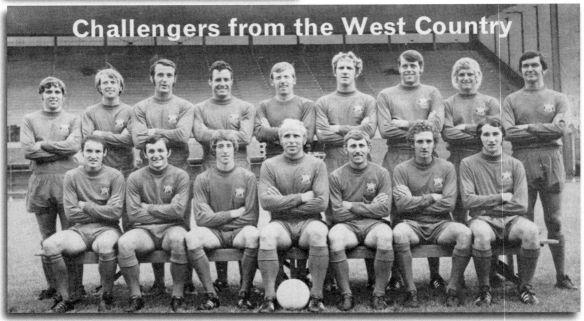

Bristol City FC 1971-72: Back row: Trevor Jacobs, Jantzen Derrick, Alan Skirton, Gordon Parr, Mike Gibson, Jack Connor, John Galley, Chris Garland, Ken Wimshurst. Front row: Danny Bartley, Trevor Tainton, Gerry Sharpe, Dickie Rooks (captain), Brian Drysdale, Geoff Merrick, Gerry Gow.

expected so late in my career and just made my short stay with Waterford all the more memorable.

What do you think of modern day football?

The game has changed so much. There is so much passing across and back, playing in little triangles today. We liked to get the ball forward or out to the wings as quickly as we could. I didn't consider myself a dirty player and never went out to kick anybody. I believe I only got into trouble with a referee once. But I did like to get stuck into what was then considered a fair tackle and I think I would find myself in a lot more bother with officials now.

TOM RITCHIE

1972-1981 & 1981-1982

Effective in midfield or attack, Tom Ritchie came down from Scotland to join City as a teenager in 1969 and went on to play in all four divisions during two memorable spells with the club. Having been top scorer in the 1975-76 promotion season, which brought top flight football to Ashton Gate, he returned after a spell at Sunderland to captain the 1983-84 side, who went up from the Fourth Division.

When you first arrived at Ashton Gate did you believe you were joining a club capable of one day playing in the First Division?

I never really thought about that to start with. When I travelled down on the train from Glasgow Central in 1969 with my brother Steve, Gerry Gow and a lad called Billy Menmuir, we were all just looking to launch professional careers. We were met at Temple Meads by John Sillett, who was assistant to manager Alan Dicks and everything developed from there. When I signed as a pro, John Galley and Chris Garland were the regular strike partnership for the first team and I was miles down the pecking order. My first aim was to become part of what became a very successful youth team under John Sillett. We reached the semi-finals of the FA Youth Cup in 1970 and I think as many as seven or eight of the side went on to play for the first team, which when you think back now was quite an achievement.

One of the young players back then was John Lillington, who went on to be club secretary at Ashton Gate after a really bad injury in the youth team finished his playing career. From Under-17 football, I gradually made my way into the reserves, who were then in the Football Combination. That meant a chance to play against top players at the likes of Tottenham Hotspur, Arsenal, Chelsea and West Ham, who were in the reserves because they were coming back after an injury. Spurs used to win the Combination regularly, but we were close up behind them for a couple of seasons. They had players like Graeme Souness and Steve Perryman coming through at the same time. I never would have thought playing against them then that we would one day all be playing in the First Division.

JOHN SHAW   KEVIN BOND   TOM RITCHIE   KEVIN REEVES

TUESDAY
APRIL 20
PORTSMOUTH
Division II
Kick-off 7.30 p.m.

Official Matchday Magazine

You made your first team debut in a home game against Millwall at the start of the 1972-73 season and at that time your position was in midfield.

Yes, I always classed myself as a midfield player, even though I went on to spend time as a striker. I remember really enjoying my debut, but then had a spell in and out of the side while I was still learning the game. Gradually, I could see things taking shape with the first team. We were becoming a tighter unit with every season. The FA Cup run in 1973-74 when we beat Leeds United before losing to Liverpool in the quarter-finals was an indication of that. By the time the 1975-76 season came along we had already pushed for promotion a couple of times and everything was in place to make it happen. Keith Fear picked up an injury and Alan Dicks asked me to have a go at playing up front beside Paul Cheesley. I particularly remember an early home game against Oxford United, which we won 4-1, with Cheese and I both scoring twice.

Our partnership really developed from there and we ended up sharing 34 goals that season. Paul's qualities suited my game and we hit it off. But there were so many other players capable of contributing goals. Gerry Sweeney got three in quick succession at a vital stage of the season to get us results against Charlton, West Brom and Sunderland, while Jimmy Mann and Gerry Gow were well capable of scoring from midfield.

What do you recall of the 1-0 win over Portsmouth that clinched City's return to the top flight of English football after an absence of 65 years?

I remember sitting in the dressing room after we had battled our way through the fans on the pitch and thinking "Crikey! We have actually done it". There had been so much anticipation and the nerves at being so close had led to us playing really poorly on the night. Clive Whitehead got the goal early on, but far from settling us, we seemed to get more jittery. I was very nervous because the target we had all been striving for was in sight. Portsmouth were already relegated and had nothing to lose. Their young team played well and we had to battle for every ball to get the victory we needed. The celebrations afterwards are a blur, apart from looking down from the stand and seeing all our fans going mad on the pitch. That was an unbelievable sight and the feelings that night are impossible to describe. It was pretty surreal when it began to sink in that we would be playing the likes of Liverpool, Manchester United and Arsenal the following season.

What are your memories of the first game in Division One at Arsenal, which kicked off the 1976-77 season?

The first thing that comes to mind was when the team coach drove down the road to Highbury, looking out of the windows and seeing the number of supporters already there. It just brought it home that this was something different. There was red and white everywhere because they were the colours of both clubs, even though we wore white shirts and black shorts for the game. It was a magical day, capped by the result. A lot of people didn't give us a chance, but when we stepped onto that pitch we didn't expect to lose. There was a lot of self-belief remaining from the previous season and we were confident of playing well, even though we were going into the unknown. As it turned out, Paul Cheesley got the only goal, but we could easily have won by three or four. I probably should have notched the winner myself because in the move that led to Cheese's goal I broke through the middle, but Sammy Nelson got back to push the ball out wide. I chased after it and laid it back to Clive Whitehead, who got in a great cross for the big fella to power home a header. I just felt "Wow! Get in there!" Clive was 'tricky-dicky' on the wing and had everything you want

to play in that position. He was a great lad to play with and made me smile, on and off the pitch.

I had a couple of other chances at Highbury that I failed to put away. Arsenal had a World Cup winner in little Alan Ball in midfield and Gerry Gow, a fantastic player to have in your side, just shone above him. Gowy, Trevor Tainton and Jimmy Mann were all superb for us in the middle of the park. We were not surprised by the result, but it gave us even more confidence going forward. Even though Cheese got injured in the next game against Stoke City, we picked up a couple of draws and then hammered Sunderland 4-1, so we were looking towards the top of the table, not the bottom.

As his partner in an increasingly successful strike-force, you must have felt the sickening blow of losing Paul Cheesley to injury more than anyone.

It was a dreadful blow for the club and I did feel it more than most because Cheese and I were just starting to learn about each other's game. Looking back now, I don't think we played more than about 40 matches together up front and the partnership was just developing. Paul frightened defenders to death in the air because he was a big powerful lad with phenomenal heading ability. But he was also deceptively quick. When he suffered the injury, jumping for a ball with Stoke goalkeeper Peter Shilton, none of us realised how serious it would prove to be. Paul was just starting to believe in himself as a player and I have no doubts that he would have gone on to play for England. When any ball was played towards him in the air, I knew he would get a flick-on and it was just a question of getting on the end of it.

He would have gained an England Under-23 cap during the promotion season had he not put club before country and played for us in a fixture that clashed with the international. It's so frustrating to think now that, with the advances in the medical side of the game that have been made over the years, Paul probably would have had 12 months on the sidelines and then returned, instead of having his career ended. Things have changed so much. We had a first team squad of only around 17 players, which meant a lot of us had to keep playing when injured. There were cortisone injections and pain-killers to keep us going, but a lot of players suffered later in life as a result.

Even now I look back and think "if only Cheese had stayed fit – what might we have achieved".

It must have been great going to play at all the First Division grounds at the time. Which one sticks out in your memory?

Playing at Highbury was very special because it was the first game and I always used to particular enjoy going to Portman Road to play Ipswich Town. But if I had to pick one of the grounds it has to be Anfield. Liverpool were the top side in Europe as well as England at the time and I can remember standing in the tunnel before the game when they emerged from the dressing room to line up alongside us. As you walked towards the entrance to the pitch you had to pass beneath this big sign with "This is Anfield" written on it. The Liverpool players all reached up and touched it as we walked out and the hairs on the back of my neck were standing on end. They also had the best player I ever played against in the First Division. Maybe I am biased because he is a fellow Scot, but Kenny Dalglish was absolutely unbelievable. I swear he had eyes in the back of his head with the vision he possessed and the awareness of what was going on around him. I felt he was a genius and he played in a great Liverpool side.

City actually beat that Liverpool team at Ashton Gate towards the end of the first season in Division One, which ended in extraordinary circumstances.

A lot of people had written off our chances of staying up, not just because we were a little way behind in the relegation battle, but also because of the teams we had to face in our last

Tom evades a challenge from Liverpool's Phil Boersma

five games, which included Manchester United and Leeds United, as well as Liverpool, at home. All of a sudden Chris Garland hit a purple patch and it was his goals that kept us up. He scored against Manchester United to earn us a 1-1 draw and then got the winner against Leeds. By the time we played Liverpool in our penultimate game they had already been crowned champions and had reached the European Cup final, so it wasn't a bad time to play them. Whether that made any difference or not, I don't give a hoot. Chris scored twice and we beat them 2-1, which gave us a fighting chance going into our final match.

That final match was against Coventry City at Highfield Road and will be remembered forever for the way it ended? What do you recall of that extraordinary evening?

I remember Coventry chairman Jimmy Hill coming into our dressing room before the game to tell us the kick-off had been put back 15 minutes because of supporters arriving late and still waiting to get into the ground. That seemed perfectly understandable to us at the time and nothing much was made of it. When the match did start we found ourselves 2-0 down early in the second half, but managed to get ourselves back in it when Gerry Gow scored. Then, with the clock running down, Donnie Gillies equalised and I firmly believe that under normal circumstances we would have gone on to win the game because the momentum was with us.

All of a sudden, the result at Everton was put up on the scoreboard and at the same time I could see Jimmy Hill on the touchline screaming that the game at Goodison was over. Sunderland had been beaten 2-0, which meant a draw was sufficient to keep both Coventry and ourselves in the First Division.

When the message got through to everyone we had the ball and no opponent came near us as we kept it in our own half. Both sets of fans were celebrating and Ray Cashley kept throwing the ball out and getting it back. There were suggestions later that Jimmy Hill rigged the late kick-off and masterminded the whole thing. But I think there were good reasons for delaying the start of the game and it was a situation that just developed on the night. I was so relieved at the outcome because I had been carrying an injury for much of the campaign and didn't have a good season.

I took a knock against Sunderland and was never quite able to shake it off. So to sit there in the dressing room, knowing I was going to get another crack at playing in Division One the following season was a good feeling. We later celebrated back at Ashton Gate and everyone was over the moon about staying up.

Three more seasons at top level followed. What made that City team so special?

From Ray Cashley to Clive Whitehead, numbers 1 to 11, and the other members of the squad of about 17, there was an abundance of talent. Many of us had been together since youth team days and by the time we played in the First Division the side had been maturing over four or five years. The lads like me, who came down from Scotland, blended in really well and added to the banter in the dressing room, but there were also a lot of Bristol lads desperate to do well for their home town club. I am Scottish through and through, but I love Bristol and Bristol City. Both have been brilliant for me and at the time there was such a close bond between the players on and off the pitch that we were able to make the absolute most of our collective talent.

There was also a trophy win when City lifted the Anglo-Scottish Cup in 1978.

There were so many stories attached to that run. We finished top of a group that also included Bristol Rovers, Plymouth Argyle and Birmingham City and then recovered a two-goal deficit from the first leg to win our quarter-final 3-2 on aggregate against Partick Thistle. That was nothing compared to the drama in the semi-final against Hibernian. The first leg was at Easter Road, where one of my old schoolteachers had once taken me to watch Hibs play against a Real Madrid side, including Ferenc Puskas. He told me I was about to watch the best team in the world. Our game there created huge headlines because both Norman Hunter and Peter Cormack were sent off, Norman for a tackle he wouldn't have thought out of the ordinary and Peter for butting one of their players in retaliation.

I found myself up front on my own when we had nine men, but we still managed a 1-1 draw. The second leg was a fantastic game, which we won 5-3, Kevin Mabbutt getting two of the goals. He also scored in the first leg of the final, which we won 2-1 at St Mirren, and again in the second leg at Ashton Gate, which ended 1-1. It may not have been the biggest competition in the world, but I remember feeling really proud that we had actually won something. St Mirren's manager at the time was a certain Alex Ferguson, who tapped me on the shoulder in the bar after the match and whispered that if ever I wanted to play back home in Scotland I should phone him. I always had a soft spot for Sir Alex from then on! Tony Fitzpatrick, who later joined City, was St Mirren captain.

You left City to join Sunderland during the season after relegation from Division One. What were the circumstances that led to the move?

I had no desire to leave Ashton Gate. But the club were keen to cash in on their saleable assets as financial problems began to surface. I had no idea how serious they would become and, had I turned down the move to Sunderland, I might well have ended up as one of the 'Ashton Eight'. Those lads who tore up their contracts were mates and I look back and think it could so easily have been me. The transfer to Sunderland didn't work out. I had a poor time in the North East and didn't do myself justice. I hold my hand up to that. When the chance came to return to City 18 months later I took it, even though by then the club had dropped into the Fourth Division and it meant taking a hefty wage cut of around 50 per cent. Terry Cooper phoned me and told me exactly what was on the table. I wouldn't have considered joining any other club for the same terms at the time, but Bristol had become home to me and my family and I wanted a new challenge. It was always our intention to return to the Bristol area at some point and instead of waiting until the end of my career I got the chance to play a few more seasons for the club I had come to love.

So, having played for City at the biggest grounds in the country, what was it like stepping out at the likes of Darlington and Hartlepool?

A real eye-opener. I remember a game at Hartlepool when we all raced off the pitch at the end to try and be first into the bath because it was so small. With 14 of us in it, there was not a lot of room! Those sort of fixtures were character-forming after the glamour of the First Division. The whole matchday experience was very different. When we were playing the likes of Arsenal and Liverpool there were cooking facilities on the team coach and one of the staff, Bill Tovey, would prepare meals like steak and eggs for the lads. In the Fourth Division it was a service station and a cup of coffee, or if we were lucky a stop at a fish 'n chip shop on the way home from away games.

City stumble to disaster

By Richard Latham

CITY FACTS

Northampton's twin strikers Massey and Syrett found room to get in 11 goal attempts between them — an in-

NORTHAMPTON 7,
BRISTOL CITY 1

SHELL-SHOCKED City players left Northampton's County Ground too stunned for words after one of the most humiliating defeats in the club's

Before we talk about your second promotion with City in 1984, there was a certain game at Northampton Town the previous season that supporters who were there will never forget.

We were beaten 7-1 and I hate to admit it, but I played that day. It was probably the lowest point in my career. I had not been back with the club long and I remember trooping of the pitch at Northampton thinking we have got a lot of work to do. It was the heaviest defeat I had ever been involved in and was very hard to take. By December that season we had dropped to the bottom of the entire Football League and every time we went out to play it was like a battle for survival. Thankfully, fortunes started to change with the turn of the year and we ended up finishing 14th with a bit of momentum to take into the following season. I can recall that by the time Terry Cooper made a few new signings I went into the 1983-84 campaign thinking it could be our season. He appointed me captain, which I will always be grateful to him for, and it was a privilege to lead that group of players.

What made the difference and tuned a bottom of the table Fourth Division side into a promotion one?

John Kerr was signed to play up front and Bruce Halliday to operate alongside big Forbes Phillipson-Masters at centre-back. Howard Pritchard returned to the club and there was a great mix of characters in the squad. Forbes was one of them, a great lad. Football-wise, he may have lacked a bit of skill, but he did a terrific job for us. Off the pitch he worked as a painter and decorator and I spent a few afternoons helping him, enjoying every minute. It gave me an indication of what life would be like without football. Then Kenny Stroud arrived and I loved playing with him in the middle of the park. We had goals in us, with the likes of Pritch, Alan Crawford and Glyn Riley, and I managed to chip in with a few from midfield (15 to be precise). When we had put ourselves in with a decent chance of going up, Terry added Trevor Morgan and Keith Curle to the squad and they strengthened us further. Even then, we only squeezed up in fourth place, Trevor's two goals at Chester clinching promotion.

That day at Chester the crowd was less than 4,000, but most of the fans seemed to have travelled from Bristol.

Yes, it was like a home game for us. When the final whistle went and we had won 2-1, our supporters raced onto the pitch and by the time the players got back to the dressing room we had very little on. The shirts had gone and so had most of the boots and socks so a lot of the fans went home with souvenirs. It was big Trevor's day as he scored twice and what a character he was on and off the pitch.

EVENING POST, TUESDAY, MAY 8, 1984 — 9

PROMOTION SPECIAL
By Bristol City reporter Richard Latham

Sing-along City back in tune

CHESTER 1, BRISTOL CITY 2

A DEAFENING roar and a sea of red-and-white scarves greeted City's triumphant return to the Third Division on a day when players and supporters were a credit to the club.

As manager Terry Cooper conducted frenzied chants of "Going Up" from the front of the Sealand Road stand, jubilant fans

CHESTER FACTS

SWINDON FACTS

Alan Crawford emerges from a sea of faces as Ashton Gate begins to celebrate after the

There was nothing remotely quiet about him and on the field he could be hilarious with some of his patter.

I can remember getting a letter from him after I had left the club for the second time. It contained a tea-bag and the message "have a drink on me". That was Trevor. The coach trip back from Chester was pretty raucous, with players taking it in turns to sing through the microphone at the front of the coach. I'm told John Shaw and I duetted on 'Miss You Nights', which must have driven everyone mad. A few drinks had gone down, but it was a great day after all the club had been through and the highlight of what was a very enjoyable second spell at Ashton Gate.

How did you find Terry Cooper as a manager?

Let's say he had a different outlook on management than I was used to. He would say things and I would think "I'm not quite sure about that". But the fans loved him and in the end he did the job that was required. I had become used to working with Alan Dicks for more than ten years at Ashton Gate and he and Terry were chalk and cheese when it came to styles of management. It was only when I left City to join Sunderland that I realised just how good AD was at his job. Terry was far more easy-going. Great player that he had been, he often used to leave the talking in the dressing room to his assistant Clive Middlemass. One big difference to Alan's days was that between them Terry and Clive had to do so many jobs outside the normal management and coaching duties because there were so few staff at the club.

You must have played in a few local derbies during your two spells with City.

Yes, and every one of them was special. Even if we were in different divisions, there were the Gloucestershire Cup finals every year and it was a buzz to play against Rovers whatever the competition. They had some very good sides during my spells with City and some fine players in the likes of goalkeeper Dick Sheppard, Frankie Prince, big Stuart Taylor and Mike Green at the back, Smash and Grab (Alan Warboys and Bruce Banister), Paul Randall and later Archie Stephens, who I regarded as a really good centre-forward. The build-up to any derby game was that bit different and we desperately wanted to win for the fans, as well as ourselves.

Mention of Archie Stephens takes us back to an FA Cup second round tie at Eastville in December 1983 when he scored for Rovers against City, but your team pulled off a shock result.

Archie wasn't a big lad, but he was deadly in the air, as we found to out cost that day. We were a division below Rovers and, with home advantage, they were widely expected to win. That looked like being the case when Archie headed a great goal to put them in front. But I remember thinking at the time that it was against the run of play and that we had been in the ascendency. It was quite late on in the game when I managed to nick the equaliser and it seemed we would be going back to Ashton Gate for a replay. That would have suited us because we would have fancied our chances of completing the job there. It didn't happen

because Terry Cooper, who had introduced himself as a substitute, played a ball down the line to Glyn Riley and he produced a bit of magic before cutting back a cross for Martyn Hirst to tap home the winner.

Martyn was a student at Bristol University and only on a part-time contract, so it was quite a day for him. My most vivid memory is of our fans celebrating at the end. They hadn't had much to cheer in recent seasons and it meant so much to them. There were a lot in the ground and a good few watching from up by the motorway which ran past the stadium. I remember looking up and seeing a crowd of them gathered there going absolutely crazy when the game ended.

Can you pick one favourite memory of your two spells with City?

There are so many. The obvious one though is turning up at Highbury for that first game in Division One. When our coach drove the last bit of the journey I thought what huge support Arsenal had because of all the red and white. The next thing all we could hear was "Bristol City" being chanted by what turned out to be our fans. They never stopped singing throughout the 90 minutes and it just made the day all the more special.

But there are countless other great memories and, when we get back together, the lads from the First Division days still talk about them and giggle about the same things that made us laugh 40-odd years ago. Sometimes I have to pinch myself over having made more than 500 appearances for the club. To be referred to as a 'legend' by the fans makes me slightly uncomfortable because it is such a huge accolade. But they were magical times for me at Ashton Gate. Bristol City is in my blood and always will be.

LEROY ROSENIOR MBE   1992-1994

Nearing the end of a top-level playing career with Fulham, Queens Park Rangers and West Ham United, Leroy Rosenior joined City in March 1992 and helped the team battle successfully for Second Division survival. Despite increasing knee problems, he was a first team regular the following season and later served the club as coach and joint caretaker-manager. He was awarded an MBE in 2018 for his work tackling discrimination in football and society in general.

What was your perception of City when you signed, having spent your career in the bright lights of London? Did you see Bristol as a footballing backwater or believe there was potential at Ashton Gate?

I signed because of the manager Denis Smith. He had tried to sign me on previous occasions when I was at West Ham so I wanted to do well for him. I also needed to be playing because I had fallen out of the first team reckoning at Upton Park. There was no way I would have passed a normal medical, but Denis pushed the move through because he needed a couple of players to help stave off relegation. I looked at the players currently at Ashton Gate and there were some experienced lads like Mark Aizlewood, Andy Leaning and Gary Shelton, who I knew were really good professionals. So, I did see potential and that was one of the reasons I signed. I wanted a new challenge and Denis sold the club to me. It was only when I moved that I realised what a magnificent place Bristol was to live in. The supporters were fantastic to me and I loved the stadium. Soon I was convinced it was a club that could go places. The one problem with Bristol being such a great area is that a lot of players over the years have focussed on that as their reason for coming here, rather than signing for football reasons.

You joined City around the same time as a certain Andy Cole.

Yes, his career was going one way and mine the other! I actually looked after Andy in our early days at the club when we both stayed at the Avon Gorge Hotel. As it turned out, he and I both got goals from the start and we managed to stay up. I got on really well with him. A lot of people found him difficult off the pitch and thought him arrogant, but that

was because he was young and basically shy. Andy had outstanding pace and was pleasing on the eye because he ran like a gazelle. He was also greedy and selfish in his desire to score goals. By the time he left City he was a very good player, but there was much more to come and he improved first with Newcastle United and then Manchester United. That was because he worked hard at his game and was a really good professional. He had a reputation for being a bad trainer while he was at Arsenal, but I always found him ready to come in early, properly prepared, and eager to work. Since we both finished playing, I have seen him a lot through media work. Before that, when my son Liam joined Fulham from City, Andy was there and looked after him, just as I had done with him at the start of his career.

Another of your regular team-mates was Jacki Dziekanowski, a real crowd favourite, but not always as popular with his fellow players. How did you feel about playing in the same side as him?

I loved Jacki as a player, but I knew that with both him and Andy Cole in the side I would have to do a lot of their work for them. I was the old guy with the dodgy knee, but I was up and down the pitch, back defending when necessary. We played as a sort of three and Jacki would always stay forward when we were defending corners. My job was to win the first ball and supply him and Andy so they could get into scoring positions. I didn't mind as long as we were getting results and sometimes I was left in awe over what they could do.

As I player, I was always happy if the other members of the team were doing their jobs. Jacki's was to get on the ball and make things happen and if he wasn't doing that I would be the first to have a go at him. Defending wasn't part of his game. But, when it comes to players I have played with and against, he was right up there with the likes of Liam Brady, Glenn Hoddle and Paul Gascoigne in terms of ability.

Do you find it sad that City have never been able to hold on to their most talented players for very long?

It's all about the level the club are playing at. We were in what is now the Championship when I was playing and someone like Andy Cole was naturally keen to play with and against the top players in the country. When Bristol City get into the Premier League, which I am convinced they will, they will start holding onto their top players. I thought it would have happened long ago, but apart from the Gary Johnson era, when they reached the Championship Play-off final and so nearly made it, they have always fallen short for one reason or another. I felt Steve Cotterill was a perfect match for City as a manager because I had competed against him when he was at Cheltenham Town and I was at Gloucester City. I knew how ambitious he was and felt he had a good young squad. Steve Lansdown is a magnificent owner and people should recognise that.

Perhaps there have been too many changes of manager over the years. Denis Smith was sacked after just ten months in charge, which must have come as a shock to you.

It did because Denis was a good man. I don't know what went on behind the scenes, but he got me involved in the coaching side at the club and I will always be grateful to him for that. In fairness to Steve Lansdown, I think he has tried to introduce greater stability by giving managers more time, perhaps in some cases too much. He wants to back the guys he has put in charge, not just financially, but emotionally as well. And he hasn't been afraid to give young managers a chance.

Your playing career at Ashton Gate ended with persistent knee problems, but you certainly went out with a bang.

Yes, in the final game of the 1992-93 season I managed to score a hat-trick against Brentford at Ashton Gate. My knee was pretty bad by then and felt very stiff. It may have been no coincidence that I was drug tested after the game. The people involved couldn't

SOCCER-SPECIAL Bristol City 4 Brentford 1

City hat-trick man breaks visitors' hearts

STUNG! ROSENIOR SWATS THE BEES

RICHARD LATHAM reports from ASHTON GATE

CITY'S end-of-season party turned into a wake for thousands of visiting supporters.

Leroy Rosenior took home the match ball in a carrier bag as souvenir of the day his hat-trick condemned Brentford to a rapid return to the Second Division.

And there was little sympathy from the former

Strikers turned snappers. Back row, left to right: Wayne Allison, Terry Connor, Leroy and Andy Cole. Front row: Jacki Dziekanowski and Nicky Morgan.

believe I had scored three goals any more than I could! I was stuck in the dressing room for hours trying to produce as urine sample. It was the right time for me to finish playing and start thinking about coaching. I became assistant to manager Russell Osman, who had taken over from Denis Smith, but soon it became clear that Clive Whitehead was better suited to that role, while I was well equipped to coach the reserves.

At the time I questioned why I was losing the assistant-manager's job, but it allowed me to concentrate on coaching young players like Louis Carey and Jason Fowler, who were just starting their careers, and I absolutely loved it. I used to stand at centre-half and get them playing around me, each of them learning from their mistakes.

I remember you once telling me on the team coach going to an away game that you wanted to be the first black manager in English football. You did the job at successfully at Torquay United, so why haven't you stayed in management?

I had a wonderful four and a half years at Torquay. We won promotion to League One and I remember getting a great reception from City fans when taking my team to Ashton Gate for the first game of the 2004-05 season, which ended 1-1. After I left Torquay, offers simply did not come along. I did go to Brentford for a short time as manager, but it proved a bad decision because at the time they had no money and the team were struggling. It

Chip off the old block – Leroy's son Liam celebrates with Lee Peacock after both had scored in the LDV Vans Trophy final victory over Carlisle United at the Millenium Stadium.

came to the point where I had to make a decision about my future, whether I wanted to pursue a coaching career in the lower leagues or go into the media. I knew I couldn't do both, so I opted to give the media a try. Fortunately, I found that I could talk football, as well as coach the game, and things worked out really well. People probably remember me best for working in the Football League Show, but that was only a small part of my job. I wrote a column for the *Bristol Post*, which I really enjoyed, and still get to see a lot of games.

People who read the column hopefully came to understand that I am really positive about Bristol Sport and want to get behind it as much as possible. This is a magnificent city, deserving of great facilities and a wonderful sporting future. I am really happy and comfortable with my media work in general, which allows me to see my family, and means I don't have as many grey hairs as some people of my age working in football!

GERRY SWEENEY

1971-1982

Gerry Sweeney joined City from Morton in 1971, helped win promotion to the First Division five years later and remained a key member of the team throughout four seasons in the top flight. The reliable right-back was one of eight players forced to tear up contracts to save the club from going out of business in 1982, but later returned to Ashton Gate as a coach.

Where did your football career start?

I had a brief spell with Celtic and then moved on to Greenock Morton where I spent four and a half very enjoyable years, playing with a great set of lads. It was a small club and on odd occasions they would find themselves short of players, so I actually played in every position while I was with them. If there was a role to fill, I would put my hand up. In the reserves I played at centre-half and centre-forward, while for the first team I played in both full-back positions, in the middle of the park and on both wings. I even played in goal for the last 20 minutes in a match against Kilmarnock.

Which position was it that attracted City to sign you?

I think it was midfield. Speaking to Tony Collins, who was then head scout at Ashton Gate, he told me he had seen me play and score in a 4-2 win over Hibernian at Easter Road. That apparently was the game that led him to recommend signing me. I think the fee was a quart of dolly mixtures! Actually, it was something like £22,500.

By the promotion season of 1975-76 you had long been a regular at right-back. But you still managed to score a few vital goals in the latter stages of that campaign.

We had been through a sticky spell around about Christmas, but started fighting back. Then came a particularly tough month of fixtures, with difficult trips to Charlton Athletic, West Brom, Sunderland and Carlisle United. We managed to beat West Brom and draw at Sunderland, who were our main rivals for promotion. At Charlton we took a point and we won at Carlisle, so it was a huge period for us. I was fortunate enough to score in three of those

games and the most talked-about goal was the one at Sunderland. People referred to it as a great volley, but what was often overlooked was that the move which led to it started with goalkeeper Ray Cashley. He threw the ball to Geoff Merrick, who then exchanges pass after pass with Gerry Gow and Brian Drysdale waiting for an opening to materialise. From Cash letting the ball go, to me receiving it, was something like 18 passes, in which I touched it twice. I had made a run from right to left when Donnie Gillies gave me the ball and I knocked it to Brian Drysdale. He returned it to me 25 yards out and I managed to find the bottom corner of the net.

As time went on, you became the team's penalty-taker, with a unique style that involved no run-up and gave supporters heart failure. How did that come about?

It started at training one day. We were due to play Bristol Rovers in the Gloucestershire Cup final, as we did every season, and coach John Sillett got the lads taking penalties, more for a bit of a laugh than anything. I just placed the ball, took half a step back and fired it into the net. The session went on for about half an hour and I think I scored ten out of ten. The reaction was "you wouldn't do that in a game", but I assured everyone that I would. There were two bits of logic involved. I didn't give the goalkeeper a chance to learn anything from my approach to the ball or where I was looking.

When I was younger I used to gaze at one corner of the net and at the very last minute change feet and aim for the other side of the goal. That worked in schoolboy football, but I tried it once as a professional and the keeper laughed at me after saving comfortably. I never got to take another penalty for Morton after that, but by the time I came to take them for City I just focused on the corner I wanted to score in and stuck to it. The one step run-up, if that what's you could call it, gave the keeper no time to move before the ball was struck and it worked pretty well.

After winning promotion, you spent four seasons locking horns with the best players in the country. What are your memories of those years?

Words fail me to describe what a high we were on as a squad after being promoted to the First Division. We weren't just playing against the best players in Britain, but some of the best in the world because at that time Liverpool were dominating Europe and Leeds United were not far behind them. At one time or another we beat both those clubs and the likes of Arsenal and Manchester United. The game against Liverpool that stands out is the one at

Gillies strikes— with £½m goal

By PETER GODSIFF

COVENTRY CITY 2, BRISTOL CITY 2

Donnie Gillies, the player whose place seemed in most jeopardy when manager Alan Dicks pondered over his team selection for this historic match, not only scored the late equaliser, but also played a part in the first goal in Bristol City's remarkable climb-back from the dead at Highfield Road.

MATCH FACTS

Entertainment rating
Sensational.

Team performance
COVENTRY — Totally committed.
CITY — Incredible!

Man of the Match
GERRY GOW — the supreme midfield battler who scored a vital first goal of the season into the bargain.

Referee
Ron Challis (Tonbridge) — Very good.

Goals
COVENTRY — Hutchison (15 mins, 52 mins).
CITY — Gow (54 mins, Gillies 79 mins).

Shots on target
COVENTRY 7 (McDonald 2, Hutchison 3, Powell 2).
CITY 6 (Mann 3, Gow, Ritchie, Gillies).

off target
COVENTRY — 3.
CITY — 5.

Fouls
COVENTRY — 26.
CITY — 24.

Bookings
COVENTRY — Wallace (retaliation, 32 mins), Yorath (dissent, 65 mins).
CITY — Sweeney (foul, 32 mins), Garland

Ashton Gate near the end of our first season in the top flight when they were the most powerful force in Europe and we needed to win to have a chance of staying up. Chris Garland scored twice and we beat them 2-1. That was quite a night.

That set you up for the final game of the season at Coventry City, which ended in extraordinary circumstances. What do you recall of that amazing evening?

We both needed a result to stay up. They went a goal up in the first half and then doubled the advantage soon after the break. If we hadn't replied quickly, all might well have been lost. But thankfully Gerry Gow pulled one back within a couple of minutes and that gave us hope.

We got a throw-in on the left-hand side, which I took, and Gowy played a one-two to get into the box before shooting home. That gave us the impetus to have a real go in the remainder of the game and, with about 11 minutes left, Donnie Gillies shot the equalizer. Then, with quite a few minutes left the scoreboard at the ground announced that Everton had beaten Sunderland, which meant that a point was enough for both ourselves and Coventry to stay up. It didn't register with all the players immediately and their big centre-forward Mick Ferguson was still charging around like a man possessed trying to cause us problems. Had Sunderland beaten Everton and our game finished 2-2, Coventry would have gone down, so he was still giving it everything. Big Norman Hunter said to him: "Look at the scoreboard, we're both okay", but he didn't believe it to start with. Norman then said: "It's on your own scoreboard, for goodness sake", but he still had to gesture to Terry Yorath on the Coventry bench, who then signaled for Ferguson to get back in his own half. From then on, Ray Cashley was getting the ball and rolling it out to me, I was doing a few keepie-uppies before giving it back to him and then he would throw it to Donnie Gillies on the other side of the pitch, where the same sort of thing happened. The Coventry lads stayed back and let us keep possession, so it was a very strange way for the match to end. I'm pretty sure the referee blew for full time a bit early out of sheer embarrassment.

After all the glory days in the First Division, you ended up as one of the Ashton Eight. When were you first aware of the dire financial problems at Ashton Gate, which brought your long City career to such a sad end?

We knew that attendances had fallen considerably following two relegations and that the club was not making much money. But none of us in our worst nightmares could have

Gerry outjumps Paul Cheesley to celebrate the big striker's winning goal against Arsenal at Highbury

imagined the circumstances that led to the departure of the 'Ashton Eight'. There was absolutely no warning as far as I was concerned. We played Aston Villa in the FA Cup on a Saturday and several of the lads got letters handed to them. I wasn't one of them and the rest of us were told to take the day off the following Monday. I still had no idea what was going on and was actually outside washing my car that day when I received a phone call telling me to come to the ground. I wanted time to change clothes, but was told not to bother and to get there as soon as possible.

When I arrived, I was met by the other players, but before much was said, one of the directors realised I was there and told us all to go back into the room where they had been talking. The conversation then carried on from where it left off prior to me joining the others and I was sitting there totally in the dark. I had to break into it to ask what the hell was happening. Only then was it laid on the line that the club was going to the wall and that we would have to tear up our contracts to stop that happening.

I looked around the room at the faces of the players because it seemed so unbelievable I thought it might have been a wind-up. Chris Garland was a funny lad and it wouldn't have surprised me if he had engineered it all as a joke. The solicitor for the club was talking and when I saw the lads were all serious, it still went through my mind that this couldn't be happening. That feeling ended when Geoff Merrick spoke up and said that the club had obviously taken advice and now we needed time to do the same by contacting the Professional Footballers Association. At one point we were given half an hour to make our minds up, but Geoff made it clear that was definitely out of the question. We asked for leave to phone the PFA and that was agreed.

Why did you not receive the same letter as other players had been given at the Villa game?

Only later when I spoke to the manager Roy Hodgson, who had not long taken over, did that become clear. He told me he was going to work as hard as possible to make the best of the situation and I said I would be only too pleased to help, but would he please tell me what had happened in my case. He made it clear the accountants had been through the books again after the original list of players was drawn up and found reason why I should be added to it. My first thought was that if the accountants were efficient why did they need to go through things a second time. My contract was not due to expire until the end of the season after the one we were involved in, so I would have been about 38 when I finished. It was bad enough for me, but lads like Chris Garland, Geoff Merrick, Trevor Tainton and David Rodgers had virtually been born with Bristol City kits on. Trevor had been in the first team for 15 years and Geoff not much less, so it must have been even more soul-destroying for them.

What was the initial reaction from the PFA?

They told us that under no circumstances should we tear up our contracts and that officials would travel down the next day. We went back to the club and its solicitors and conveyed that message, making it clear we would do nothing until we had spoken to PFA representatives in person. Sure enough, officials did arrive the following day and met us at the ground. They then advised us not to take things any further until their solicitors had met with those representing the club. Days went by with our situation no clearer and several of us actually played the following Saturday at Newport County in a League game that ended 1-1. By then the media were all over the story and when it became known that the club would only survive if we tore up our contracts, Chris Garland started getting threats that he had better do it, or he and his family would suffer. I don't know how serious the warnings were, but it was a terrible time. In fact, there was not one argument between the eight players over what the right course of action was going to be. We all stuck together when we played football and it was the same off the pitch, even in these extraordinary circumstances.

So let's come on to decision day and the meeting at the Dragonara Hotel in Bristol on February 3rd 1982 when everything came to a head. What do you remember of that day?

Before going to the Dragonara, we had got together and decided that the club had to survive, no matter what. We all had mortgages to pay and in some cases school fees, which were real worries, but the PFA had agreed with the new board about to take over the club that a match would be organised, with the gate takings split between us, which was something. Ahead of the final meeting, we agreed that for the sake of the supporters and the other people working at Ashton Gate, Bristol City had to have a future. We were never given the alternative of playing for less money, so it was sacrifice our contracts or have no club to employ us anyway. There came a moment at the Dragonara when we actually had to sign away our

The 'Ashton Eight' – clockwise from top: Peter Aitken, Chris Garland, Geoff Merrick, David Rodgers, Jimmy Mann, Julian Marshall, Gerry and Trevor Tainton.

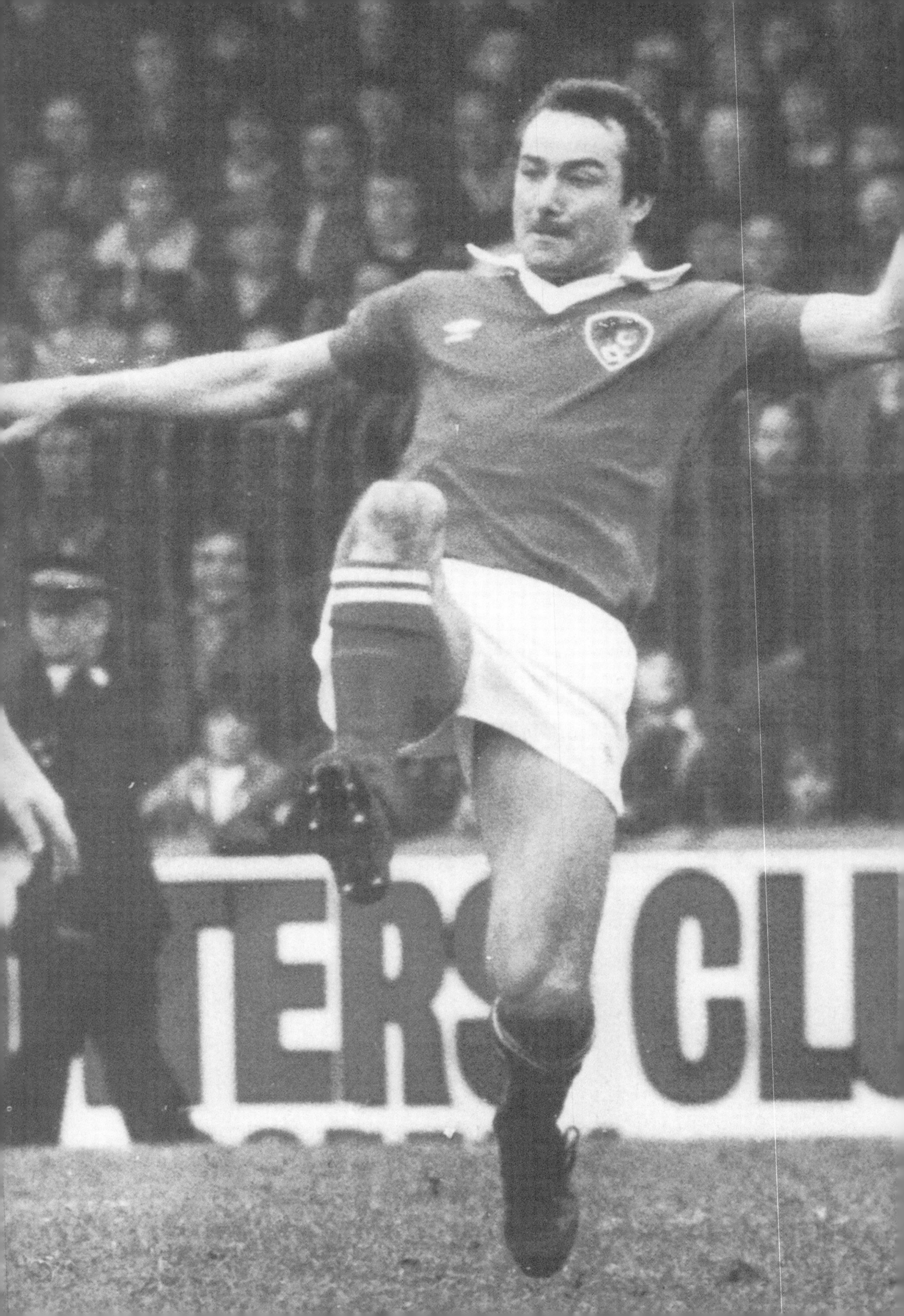

futures, but while there was anger and resentment, we knew it was the only step to take. Some people suggested that we had been paid too much, but player wages back then were nothing like they are today. They were decent, but in no way set you up for life, so it was clear we would all have to get jobs of some sort to support our families.

Did it affect some of you more than others?

Well I was one of the older ones. I joined York City for the rest of the season and that was me finished as a player. Peter Aitken came with me, while Chris Garland and Geoff Merrick went to play abroad for a while. I am not sure what happened with the others, but it was a devastating blow to us all. A couple of years earlier we had been playing in the top flight of English football against the likes of Liverpool and Manchester United and here we were out of work, through no fault of our own.

When you drive past Ashton Gate now and see the super stadium it has become, with Championship crowds of over 20,000, surely you can't help reflecting on the unfairness of what happened.

No, I am glad the club survived and is thriving. I had and still have a huge affection for the fans, who work hard and deserve to have a decent team to support. They were the main reason we took the decision we did in 1982 and now I am one of them. I returned to work for City as a coach, which I wouldn't have done if I had felt any bitterness. I did hear that at an early board meeting following our departure as players it was suggested we might be given season tickets for life and the motion was rejected. If so, that's a bit disappointing, but there is a plaque at Ashton Gate recognising what we did and I am not the sort to bear grudges. I am sorry about what happened, but glad we acted appropriately and I am a City fan for life.

TREVOR TAINTON

1967-1982

Trevor Tainton joined City from school and went on to make more than 550 appearances for his local club, a record bettered only by Louis Carey and John Atyeo. A versatile midfielder, who could also operate on the wing and at full-back, he played 15 seasons for the Robins, including four in the top flight of English football, before becoming one of the Ashton Eight.

You had a wonderful long career at Ashton Gate. How did it all start?

It began back in the early Sixties. I played for Bristol Boys, as well as some local sides and Stockwood Wanderers across the other side of town. In those days, you played for one team in the morning and another in the afternoon. Two games in one day and there was no rotating of any players! On several occasions, I saw City scouts Jock Rae and Cliff Morgan watching from the sidelines.

I left school in 1962, at the age of 15, and signed for the club, which was a dream fulfilled as I had been a supporter throughout my boyhood. Arsenal were apparently also interested in me, but I had no wish to leave my family or home town. In my early days at Ashton Gate, the manager Fred Ford used to pick me up along with some other lads and take us to training. His club car was a Morris 1000, which he used to drive all over the country. He would never talk football when we were in it, either on the way to training or the return journey. All he used to say was: "Cheerio, see you tomorrow", but he was a smashing chap and it said a lot about him that he was prepared to put himself out in that way for young players. Back then, chairman Harry Dolman had his factory on Pennywell Road and I went to work there as an apprentice electrician because my parents were keen for me to get a trade behind me in case my football career didn't work out. I stayed at the factory for around 18 months, but hated working indoors and always wanted playing football to be the life for me. My first contract with City was for £8 a week. I was rubbing my hands when Fred asked me if I wanted to sign and my answer was: "Yes please".

I went into the youth team and eventually made my first team debut against Carlisle United in 1967. Trevor Jacobs and a couple of other local lads were in the team that day and I really enjoyed it.

You used to wear the number seven shirt. But how many appearances for City were in the middle of the park and how many on the wing?

I started off in central midfield, which I always felt was my best position, but I played in the reserves for several years under coach John Sillett and he asked me if I fancied playing on the wing. I told him I was happy to do anything to help the team and thoroughly enjoyed the switch. I also played at full-back, which I also liked, and after that I went back to playing in midfield again.

City struggled in the Second Division for a number of seasons after Alan Dicks became manager. When did you first get an idea that he was building something special?

We actually went pretty close to promotion for a couple of years before we actually achieved it in 1976. There was a growing feeling that we were going to reach the First Division as time went by and the mixture of mainly local lads and players brought down from Scotland gelled into a winning team. By the time the promotion season came around we all knew each other's game inside out and that was important to our success. Alan Dicks was a good motivator, who didn't have a lot of money to spend, but ensured that all the players got on with one another by taking us on pre-season tours, which were good bonding experiences. We became a closely-knit group on and off the pitch.

Who were the key players and the ones you enjoyed playing alongside most?

I would have to start with the midfield because that was my department and I got to know those alongside me really well. The first name that always comes to mind is Gerry Gow, who was a fantastic player. He was hard as nails in the tackle, but he could also pass the ball and score goals, so he had everything. Like all the Scots lads, he was very demanding of the players around him and wasn't slow to let you know if you made a mistake. But that came from his own desire to achieve success, which rubbed off on everyone. It takes all sorts to make a successful team and we had a really good blend. The Scots could run all day and we had goalscorers in Tom Ritchie and Paul Cheesley, which is vital for any good side. But our real strength was as a collective, rather than down to any one individual. We supported each other through thick and thin.

What are your most vivid memories of that time in the mid-1970s?

Something that really sticks in my mind was that first game after winning promotion against Arsenal at Highbury. It will stay with me long after the later troubles I had to endure with Bristol City are forgotten. All the hard work we had put in over several seasons had brought us to the point where we were facing one of the top clubs in the country at one of the most famous stadiums. Their team was full of household names and we managed to beat them deservedly. What a feeling that was! Sadly, a few days later Paul Cheesley, who was so important to us, suffered the knee injury against Stoke City that was to effectively end his career. I had seen the same thing happen to Gerry Sharpe earlier in my City career at a time when he was earning a lot of praise and I honestly believe Paul would have gone on to play for England had he stayed fit. He was so strong in the air, had two good feet and was quick. It was such a shame that he couldn't fulfill his potential and a hammer blow to the team.

That opening season in the First Division reached the most dramatic of conclusions in the final game at Coventry City, which crucially kicked off late to get all the fans in. How do you recall that unforgettable night?

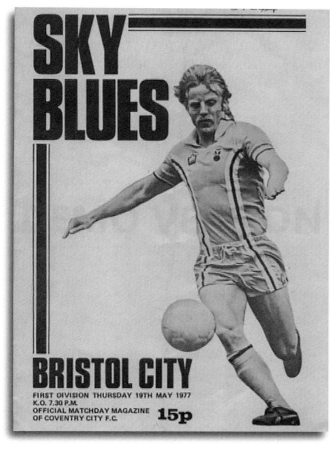

It was a really strange game to be involved in. Both teams knew a point would keep them up if Sunderland lost and, while Coventry went 2-0 up, we got it back to 2-2 and were on top. The scoreboard then informed everyone that Everton had beaten Sunderland and there were shouts from the staff on the sidelines not to do this or that to risk defeat. As time ran down, it became a case of one team holding onto the ball without venturing forward and the other sitting back. All the players involved had given their best on the night, but now common sense took over and both sets of fans were celebrating before the ref blew the final whistle. In a way, that result was just as important to us as the win that had clinched promotion a year earlier.

159

You had played against the best players in the country that season. Who stood out?

The hardest opponent I played against was Graeme Souness at Liverpool, who had similar attributes to Gerry Gow in that he could see a pass, had the ability to deliver it and scored goals. The other guy who comes to mind is Johnny Giles at Leeds United, Like his team-mate Billy Bremner, he was only small, but as well as being very talented, did not hesitate to put his foot in when necessary. The two of them together were formidable and you knew you had been in a game against them.

Talking of Liverpool, was it true you might have moved to Anfield around that time?

I will never know. There were stories going around that they were interested in signing me, but when I went in to see Alan Dicks about it, he put the shutters up and told me there was nothing in it. I accepted what he said and just got on with my job of playing for Bristol City. Maybe if it had been in the days of agents, mine would have been up at Anfield negotiating. But you never know what might have happened. I could have gone there and not played many games or ended up a European Cup winner. At the end of my career I did sort of wonder what if . . .

It was so sad to see your long City career end as one of the Ashton Eight and you were affected as badly as anyone by the club's financial collapse.

Yes, I not only lost my job, but my family business outside football and my house. I had two young sons to bring up at the time, aged nine and five, and had to look after them while being made bankrupt later that year. It was a terrible time and really hard to take after so many years with City. I went to play for Torquay United and stayed until the end

The Ashton Eight pictured at a 25th anniversary reunion. Back row, left to right: Peter Aitken, Julian Marshall, David Rodgers, Geoff Merrick. Front row: Gerry Sweeney, Trevor, Chris Garland, Jimmy Mann.

of the season. After that I went to Trowbridge Town for a couple of years before dropping into the Western League with Odd Down. When football is in your blood, it is so hard to contemplate anything else and I kept playing for as long as I possibly could.

All eight of us had our own personal lives and everything that went with them. It was such a hard time for me that I sometimes look back and think how on earth did I come through it. When we were initially told by the City directors that the club was in trouble, they said that if things came to the point they did, we would all be paid pound for pound on our contracts. That never happened. In the end we were given around £2,500 each as a result of the game that was staged to raise money for us, along with a bit of holiday pay, but nothing like what we were owed.

We were pushed into a corner and there was a lot of ill-feeling. Players were threatened because other people at the club thought they were going to lose their jobs if we didn't comply with what was needed to keep Bristol City in existence. Yet, all we wanted to do was fulfil our contracts and continue doing our best for the club. There were so many appearances between us and it was particularly hard to take for those of us who had worn the red shirt with pride from youth team days. All I ever wanted to do was play for City and, thinking back all these years later, I still get a buzz remembering what it was like. They say time is a great healer and theirs is still the first result I look for on the TV each Saturday.

While I deeply regret how it all ended for me and the other lads concerned, I still have great pride in being so high on the list of City appearance-makers. I remember playing my 500th game and thinking what an achievement that was for a Bristol boy. Had things worked out differently when I still had 18 months left on my contract I might have got closer to Louis Carey and John Atyeo. But it wasn't to be.

MICKY TANNER

1985-1987

A graduate from local club soccer, Bristolian Micky Tanner had established a reputation as a tough-tackling midfielder when he signed for City, intially as a part-timer, and then as a professional during the 1985-86 season. He is also well known for having represented a host of West country non-League clubs.

How did your transition from local club soccer to professional football come about?

One of the Bristol City directors at the time was Bob Boyd, who was always nudging Terry Cooper to look at non-League players. He had played semi-professional football himself and had a wide knowledge of the game at grass roots level. It was Bob who first approached me to ask if I fancied a trial, telling me he thought I would do really well. At first, I declined because I had been with City as a kid and absolutely fell to pieces when they let me go.

I started playing for local teams, but my heart wasn't really in it until a friend joined Hallen, who were then in the Gloucestershire County League, and urged me to go there with him. They treated me like a son and I regained my appetite for playing football. My confidence grew, with Frank and Francis Fairman taking me under their wing, and I felt like a proper person again. I had a golden period of form when everything seemed to go for me and couldn't wait for Saturdays to come along.

After a while, I phoned Bob Boyd and everything went from there. I played three trial games for City in the annual Fry's tournament and after the third Terry Cooper told me he wanted to sign me. I explained that I was doing an engineering apprenticeship, which I wanted to complete, and he said that was no problem because I could train in the evenings with Mike Gibson and Dave Caines.

They got me fitter, but it was a huge step up. The first pre-season I did, Terry took us to an RAF camp at Hullavington, where the training nearly killed me. After three days I was literally begging his assistant Clive Middlemass to let me go home. He told me to go and see physio Alex Lockhart and somehow I managed to get through it. Once the week was over, I was so fit that I felt I could run through a brick wall.

I made my first team debut in a Third Division match at Wigan Athletic during the 1985-

163

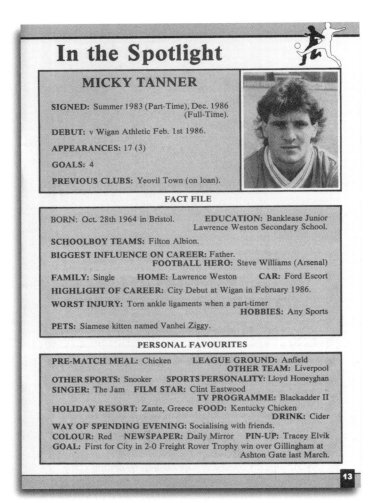

In the Spotlight

MICKY TANNER

SIGNED: Summer 1983 (Part-Time), Dec. 1986 (Full-Time).

DEBUT: v Wigan Athletic Feb. 1st 1986.

APPEARANCES: 17 (3)

GOALS: 4

PREVIOUS CLUBS: Yeovil Town (on loan).

FACT FILE

BORN: Oct. 28th 1964 in Bristol.　**EDUCATION:** Banklease Junior Lawrence Weston Secondary School.

SCHOOLBOY TEAMS: Filton Albion.

BIGGEST INFLUENCE ON CAREER: Father.
　FOOTBALL HERO: Steve Williams (Arsenal)

FAMILY: Single　**HOME:** Lawrence Weston　**CAR:** Ford Escort

HIGHLIGHT OF CAREER: City Debut at Wigan in February 1986.

WORST INJURY: Torn ankle ligaments when a part-timer
　HOBBIES: Any Sports

PETS: Siamese kitten named Vanhei Ziggy.

PERSONAL FAVOURITES

PRE-MATCH MEAL: Chicken　**LEAGUE GROUND:** Anfield
　OTHER TEAM: Liverpool

OTHER SPORTS: Snooker　**SPORTS PERSONALITY:** Lloyd Honeyghan

SINGER: The Jam　**FILM STAR:** Clint Eastwood
　TV PROGRAMME: Blackadder II

HOLIDAY RESORT: Zante, Greece　**FOOD:** Kentucky Chicken
　DRINK: Cider

WAY OF SPENDING EVENING: Socialising with friends.

COLOUR: Red　**NEWSPAPER:** Daily Mirror　**PIN-UP:** Tracey Elvik

GOAL: First for City in 2-0 Freight Rover Trophy win over Gillingham at Ashton Gate last March.

13

86 season because of an injury to skipper Bobby Hutchinson. His were big shoes to fill and it was wonderful that the manager had such faith in me.

Was it always your ambition to play for the club?

Yes, when I was a boy all I thought about was playing for Bristol City. So, when they decided not to keep me on I went through a really bad time. I was gutted and my world fell apart. If I'm honest, I went off the rails and it was only when I joined Hallen that I started getting back on my feet. It was such a lovely club, with brilliant facilities. Even so, the thought of signing for City was by then the last thing on my mind. When the opportunity came along, I hesitated because I felt they had let me down once. When I agreed to sign, none of my mates could believe it and I had to pinch myself. It was sheer joy. I was actually going to get paid to play. I negotiated my first contract with Terry Cooper and it's hard to believe but I refused his first three offers. The money had to be better than I was earning from engineering. Finally, TC came up with a deal that suited me. What he didn't know was that I would probably have played for City for nothing, just to put the shirt on, had I not known they were willing to pay me.

You always loved a tackle and when you joined Yeovil Town on loan during the 1986-87 campaign the manager there was Gerry Gow. Did you learn a lot from him?

Gerry was my idol when I watched City as a kid, so the chance to go and play for him at a time when City Reserves were in the Western League was fantastic for me. Without sounding arrogant, I was developing quickly and needed to play regularly at a higher level. When I joined Yeovil in what is now the National League, they had some good players. Alan Pardew was in midfield and both Tom Ritchie and Donnie Gillies, who had played for City in the First Division, were also part of the squad. I had a really good spell there, scoring seven goals in eight games, and the home crowds were over 3,000, compared to the man and his dog who were watching City Reserves. It was a real buzz playing for Yeovil against the likes of Wycombe Wanderers and I loved my time there. Gerry liked me as a player and gave me free rein to play my sort of game. It got around that I was playing well and City recalled me to be part of the first team squad.

Just when it seemed you were establishing yourself in City's team you were sent off in a match at Brentford. What do you recall of that day?

It remains one of my biggest regrets. I was so fired up for the game because we needed a result to boost a promotion challenge. I pushed the ball through midfield and already had it in mind that I wanted to get it out to Alan Walsh on the left wing. As I went to do so, one of the Brentford players was pulling me back and I think I connected with an elbow in trying to fend him off. The referee was right on the spot and, while I was expecting a yellow card, he sent me off. I had go down the tunnel, which was in amongst the Brentford fans, so you can imagine how hostile they were. We drew the game 1-1 after being ahead and the first player to come up to me as I was in the bath after it finished was David Moyes. He said: "The gaffer is not happy. Keep your mouth shut and take it on the chin." Terry Cooper skipped the normal team-talk and came straight to me. His language was unprintable, but you get the idea. I felt as though I had cost us the game. I lost my place in the team as a result of the suspension that followed and that hurt even more. I could take a ticking-off from the manager, but being back in the reserves was very hard to take.

Let's talk about happier occasions. You scored against Gillingham in the Freight Rover Trophy run that took City to a second Wembley appearance in 1987 and in a local derby win over Bristol Rovers.

The Gillingham game was probably the highlight of my City career and all my days playing football. It was at Ashton Gate and, having been in the squad for the earlier rounds, I got the nod to start. I was really up for it and just walking out in front of 10,000 supporters gave me goose bumps. The adrenalin was pumping and it was a day when it seemed I could do no wrong. I had been given my orders, which were basically to break up the midfield and give the ball to one of our more talented players like Rob Newman or Joe Jordan. David Moyes had given us the lead, scoring from about two yards out, so even he couldn't miss! Then we got a free kick on the halfway line, which was played into the box where Big Joe won the first header. I won the second and got the ball down, pulling it to one side and hitting it without having time to think.

It was with my left peg and the shot beat a former Bristol Rovers goalkeeper in Phil Kite. I didn't see the ball hit the back of the net because there were bodies in the way, but the crowd went nuts and it was the most deafening sound I had ever heard. All the lads jumped on me and I was in shock. It was the most amazing feeling.

That game will live in my memory forever. I don't remember as much about the Gloucestershire Cup win over Rovers, except that it was at Twerton Park and we beat them 2-1. There were only around 1,300 people watching on a really cold night, but my goal still meant the world to me. I had scored against the Rovers, we lifted the Gloucestershire Cup, and I still have my winners' trophy up in the loft.

Bristol City FC, 1987/88. Back row, left to right: Lee Rogers, Micky Tanner, Gary Marshall, Rob Newman, Paul Fitzpatrick, Keith Waugh, Mark Coombe, David Moyes, Keith Curle, Alan Walsh, Chris Honor, Russell Bromage. Front row: Tony Caldwell, Mark Cooper, Nigel Hawkins, Steve Galliers, Gordon Owen, Andy Llewellyn, Steve Neville and Joe Jordan.

You were in the squad for the Freight Rover final against Mansfield Town in 1987, but didn't make the team or the bench. That must have been hugely disappointing.

Yes, I was left out when we got to Wembley because Terry Cooper said he wanted to go with experience in midfield (Rob Newman and Alan Walsh played there). I was upset and remember going up to the VIP bar with Trevor Morgan to drown my sorrows once I knew I was not going to be in the dressing room. We watched the match from there. Trevor had been injured, but I was fully fit and gutted that Terry didn't think I was quite up to playing in such a big game. I protested that surely I was worth at least a place on the bench, but he wouldn't have it. There were only two substitutes allowed in those days. If the match had been played with today's rules I would have been part of it all. When we lost on penalties, it completed a bad day all round for me.

How did you come to leave City and start what proved a long spell of playing non-League football?

I have to admit that it was down to my own actions that I finished at Ashton Gate. My disciplinary record was poor and I had a few scrapes with referees, with a couple of red cards in the reserves. After one reserve game, an opposing player wanted to take me to court over a challenge I made on him. I didn't think it was that bad and it ended up being sorted, with nothing bad happening. But I think the directors got fed up with the bad publicity and told Terry Cooper that it just wasn't good enough. He told me Bath City wanted to sign me and that I should take up their offer because it was good money. They had just sold Paul Bodin to Newport County for £16,000 and were ready to use the cash to sign me. I still had eight months on my City contract and the other lads were telling me to see it out. But Terry made it clear there was no way back and it was a very good offer from Bath, so I decided to go there. My thinking was that if I played well enough I might get back into League football.

It didn't work out that way. It's not as easy as you think to drop into non-League after playing for a professional club, particularly one as big as Bristol City. I thought I would adapt to the different level, but I was wrong. Although the other Bath lads were great to me and I enjoyed being with them, I didn't play well and it was a difficult time. The move simply didn't work out.

After that you played for a whole host of non-League clubs. Give us a brief run-down of who they were.

When I left Bath, manager John Murphy signed me for Cheltenham Town. My form picked up again and I absolutely loved the place. I was top scorer and gained selection for the England non-League squad. We were well placed in the Conference and played some great football. Everything was going well until we were beaten 3-0 by Gloucester City in an FA Cup tie and John Murphy walked out. I didn't see eye-to-eye with his replacement and things started to go downhill. That was when my hero Gerry Gow stepped in again and signed me for Weymouth. I told him how much money I wanted, he agreed and I put in a transfer request. Gerry knew what I was like on the field and off it.

He wanted me to give his side a spark and I really enjoyed my time there. It was a pleasure playing for him. What a great man. Then the club went into financial difficulties and paid me off, after which I had a short spell at Exeter City with Terry Cooper again. I played in the pre-season friendlies and thought a contract would be put on the table, but that didn't prove the case and I went back to Bath. While there I had a few family problems and decided to give up playing football altogether.

But that wasn't the end. I came back and played local football for Sea Mills, while also helping out at a couple of other clubs, and ended up at Shirehampton. We won a league while I was there, but I was starting to pick up a few niggles and eventually had to hang up my boots. I went on to be manager of Shirehampton and won a league and cup double with them, which I still take great pride in.

BRIAN TINNION

Born in County Durham, Brian Tinnion played for Newcastle United and Bradford City before moving to Ashton Gate in March 1993. He made more than 450 League appearances for the Robins and scored one of the most famous goals in the club's history to knock Liverpool out of the 1993-94 FA Cup before later serving as manager and in key positions in the club's Academy.

You were in the same Newcastle United youth team as Paul Gascoigne. What are your memories of him at that early age?

We had a really good side and Gazza was as mad as ever. What an incredible talent. From the age of 14, I played in the same team as him and no one could ever touch him in terms of ability. At every level through to the first team he shone and continued to do so for many years after that. He always loved a laugh and a prank and was a great lad to be with. I played in the game against Wimbledon when the famous photo was taken of Vinnie Jones grabbing a certain part of Gazza's anatomy. It was always a tough place to go, but none of the other players knew until we saw the newspapers the next day what Vinnie had actually done. From the expression on Gazza's face, it looked a pretty sore one!

After moving from Newcastle to Bradford City, you joined Bristol City for £180,000. Money very well spent as it turned out.

I'll leave that for other people to decide. I think I played 551 games including cup matches over many years and I wouldn't change a thing because I enjoyed every single moment.

For all your years of service with City, you will always be best remembered as a player for a split second at Anfield on January 25th 1994 when you struck the winning goal against Liverpool in the FA Cup. What a night that must have been.

It was amazing. We had drawn 1-1 at Ashton Gate after the floodlight failure caused the first game to be abandoned and no one outside the club gave us a chance in the replay.

So it was a case of going to Anfield and trying to enjoy the experience. Liverpool had a team full of international players, but we played really well on the night and could have had more than the one goal. Around 10,000 of our supporters made the trip, which ensured us of great backing and we rose to the occasion. A lot of fans have told me since that it was an evening they will never forget. In the days after the game I actually also received a number of letters from Liverpool supporters thanking me for ending Graeme Souness' spell as manager. Not nice, but one of those things. As for my goal, the ball broke to me from Wayne Allison's run and I remember looking up and seeing Neil Ruddock and Steve Nicol coming in from the side to tackle me. That made me take the shot quickly because I thought one of them was about to smash me in two! Neil never took too many prisoners, but I just got to the ball in time and managed to bend it around Bruce Grobbelaar's outstretched right hand as he dived.

You were part of the 1997-98 promotion team under John Ward. What are your memories of that campaign?

It was great. We didn't start the season well and were under a bit of pressure because the

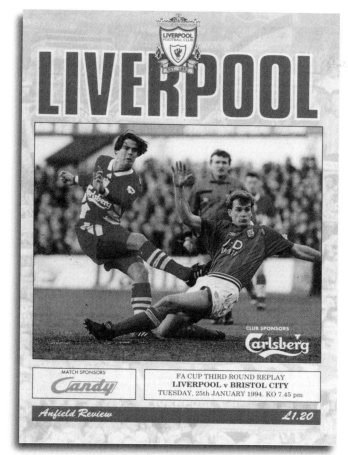

fans weren't happy. But then we went on a fantastic run and a brilliant team spirit developed. We had Shaun Goater to score the goals and Shaun Taylor at the back with Louis Carey alongside him. They were key to us having a very good team and we all stuck together, even if things were going against us. We got promoted and I still believe that squad would have gone on to even better things had the board not taken the decision to let John Ward leave and replace him with Benny Lennartsson.

How big a shock to the players was John Ward's departure less than three months into the season after the promotion campaign?

We had beaten Bolton Wanderers 2-1 in a Friday night game televised live by Sky and everyone was on a high because they had just come down from the Premier League and were among the favourites to win the Division One title. Before we knew it John Ward had lost his job. Our position in the table was okay and we weren't adrift in any sense so it was unbelievable really. There were no issues with any of the players and the spirit in the camp was still high. Benny Lennartsson took over and the effect on the lads was clear from his first two games in charge. We lost 5-0 at Bradford City and then 6-1 at home to Wolves. After those shocks, we never really recovered and ended up getting relegated. Looking back, I think we would have survived comfortably and pushed on to even better things had John Ward remained in charge.

It took a long time for the club to win promotion again, but during the intervening years there was the LDV Vans Trophy success under Danny Wilson.

To win any cup competition is a thrill and that one is very much for the fans. We took a huge contingent to the Millennium Stadium for the game against Carlisle United and the ground seemed pretty much packed. Lee Peacock and Liam Rosenior got the goals and it was another fantastic day. It's incredible when you see the joy on the fans' faces and realise you have done something to help put it there. We were expected to win, but no team is going to lie down in a cup final and we had to work hard to make our quality tell.

You succeeded Danny Wilson as manager in 2004 and had a decent first season in charge. Among other things, you gave opportunities to a lot of young players.

Yes, it was always my intention to give youth a chance and in the latter days of my playing career I watched with interest as a really good group developed and matured. We had Leroy Lita up front and the likes of Dave Cotterill, Ryan Harley and Cole Skuse, who all went on to have good careers. I firmly believed in giving players from our own Academy every chance to play in the first team and had a lot of faith in that group. It is no good having good coaches and talented young players if the first team manager is not prepared to play them. If you don't give them an opportunity, how do you know if they are good enough?

How did your many years of service with City's Academy come about?

While I was still playing, from the age of around 28, I spent a lot of time at the Academy doing some coaching because I have always been interested in the development of young players. I used to watch the various age-group teams play and take note of the lads I felt had a chance of a professional career. One was Scott Golbourne, who went on to play for the first team. I could see he was a good athlete, with a decent left foot and the energy to get about the pitch. Later, when I became City manager, I was able to give him his League debut, which gave me great satisfaction. And when the chance came to sign Scott again in 2016 I was asked for my opinion and provided a good reference to director of football Keith Burt and caretaker manager John Pemberton. By then Scott had experience of playing in the Championship and I knew he would be good for the dressing room, as well as the team.

Explain the duties involved in being Head of Youth Recruitment.

I have the final say on all players in the Academy who get signed or released when it comes to scholarships. It's a great job. We are concentrating hard on the Bristol area to make sure we get the best of our own crop before we look anywhere else and over the past 12 months we have managed to recruit 27 local players for our squads between the ages of 12 to 16. I am very hands-on and I think I went to 290 games last season alone to try and identify talented lads. It works out that I cover about eight matches a week. I absolutely love the challenge of finding the next youngster who is going have a real impact on the first team and help take the club forward.

What are you looking for in a young player to make them worthy of a place in the Academy?

They need to have heart and desire. I think football has lost the plot a bit about what is required to be a player. You can have all the ability in the world, but if you haven't got the drive to go with it the chances are you won't make it as a professional footballer. You need to have the right work ethic and maintain it at training day-in, day-out. Over the course of my own playing career, I saw a lot of talented youngsters, who didn't have the commitment to put the hard work in that is necessary to succeed in a very tough and competitive business. If you find a boy with the necessary determination to improve, then you know he has half a chance. Joe Bryan was a good example. He was a winner from a very early stage and mentally tough even at the age of 12. One summer when the first team players were off, Joe was at the Academy working on the track with one of our sports scientists. That suggests a dedicated, driven person and you could see it in the way he played. We need more like him.

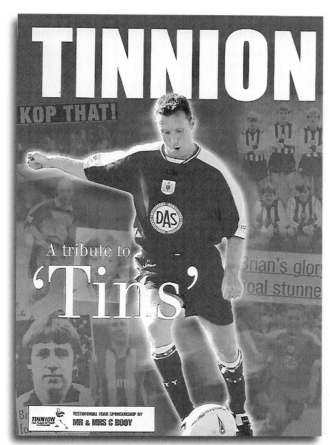

The cover of Brian's testimonial brochure

You don't actually coach at the Academy, even though there is surely a lot you could teach the young players.

No, but I talk to them a lot. I tell them what is expected of a professional footballer, the demands involved, and what they need to give up in order to achieve their ambitions. If they want to go out with their mates on a Friday night before a Saturday game, the likelihood is that they can forget about a career in football. There are all sorts of standards they need to meet and if I can help them do so by offering information gained from my own experience, then great. I daren't tell them what Gazza used to do at their age because he wasn't a great model in that way. But he had enough ability to succeed in spite of himself and very few are that gifted.

Brian flanked by City starlets Lloyd Kelly (left) and George Dowling

Even when you scout a young player and think you have found a jewel, he can be snatched away by another club. That must be hugely frustrating.

It certainly is. Everyone is looking for that one lad who stands out and competition is fierce. Since Jamie Vardy came to the fore at Leicester City, everybody is looking to non-League football for someone of similar ability who has slipped through the net of the professional clubs. We were close to getting a very good young striker from Dorchester and had the first offer in to sign him. When we talked to him one morning he didn't have an agent, but by the evening he did have one and suddenly four other clubs were interested. That killed us on that particular deal and in general we prefer to get boys in between the ages of eight and ten to make sure they are in our system so we don't have to worry about other clubs pinching them, unless they want to pay compensation. The ideal is for them to progress through our age group teams. I tend to concentrate on the Under-14s upwards and at the moment particularly between the Under-16s and Under-

21s because there have been some gaps that needed filling in certain positions. When that happens we do have to go out and recruit from other clubs at a more advanced age. I wouldn't do that if it blocked the path of a talented youngster already in our system, but sometimes it is necessary to bring someone in to help the lads already here.

We have seen you at a lot of local non-League fixtures, so clearly you believe there are capable youngsters involved in them.

Yes, definitely. I can assure lads playing even at the lower levels that we are out there looking and will keep monitoring them if they impress us. There are always late developers and we will find them and give them an opportunity if we can. We are a development football club and we want our Academy to be successful. Steve and Jon Lansdown are very keen to see local youngsters progress into the first team squad and it is my challenge to bring them into and through our youth system. We have a few Welsh boys and one or two signed from other clubs, but the majority are from this area and that's how we want it to be. The thought of one day sitting in the stand at Ashton Gate and watching some of them in first team shirts is what drives me every day.

ALAN WALSH

1984-1989

Having established himself as the top scorer in Darlington's history with 100 League and cup goals, Alan Walsh joined City for a bargain £18,000 fee, set by a Football League tribunal in July 1984. He went on to add 99 more career goals during five seasons at Ashton Gate, many of them thrilling strikes from distance with his trusty left foot.

Let's talk about City's fantastic League Cup run to the semi-finals as a Third Division club in 1988-89, which involved some memorable nights at Ashton Gate.

The best was probably the 4-1 third round win over Crystal Palace, who were a division above us and had players like Mark Bright and John Salako up front. They were going well at the time and we absolutely took them to the cleaners. Ralph Milne, God Bless Him, had a great night, which probably had a lot to do with him later earning a move to Manchester United. He scored twice and after 20-odd minutes we were 3-0 up. The atmosphere was unbelievable and I managed to get a fourth late on with a rare header! Palace got one back in the last minute, scored by Alan Pardew, who later became a successful manager, but it was a big win that gave us confidence for the later rounds. Then there was a really tight fourth round tie at home to Fourth Division Tranmere Rovers. They gave us a tough game, but Carl Shutt scored a great goal and it proved enough to put us through to the quarter-finals.

You drew Bradford City away in the last eight and took 3,000 fans to Valley Parade where your early goal proved the winner. What do you remember of that game?

We travelled up the day before and stayed at Harrogate. Bradford had caused a couple of shocks themselves in the competition, but this time were favourites. I remember Jimmy Lumsden, who was then assistant to manager Joe Jordan, coming in while we were having our pre-match meal and saying: "Hey lads, I've just been told Bradford have booked their hotel for the semi-finals." It was probably only kidology, but it fired us up and I scored in the first couple of minutes. A cross came in and I swung my left foot at the ball, which

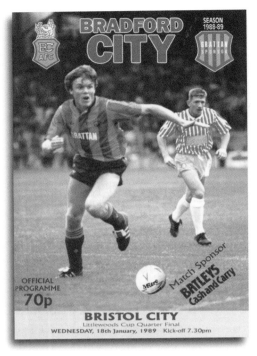

OFFICIAL PROGRAMME
70p

BRISTOL CITY
Littlewoods Cup Quarter Final
WEDNESDAY, 18th January, 1989   Kick-off 7.30pm

ended up in the bottom corner. After that it was like The Alamo and our goalkeeper Keith Waugh had a blinder. Everything they hit at him was either down his throat or he somehow managed to block the ball. We defended like Trojans and eventually got the result we wanted.

Joe Jordan came out of semi-retirement from playing to lead the attack that night and was soon showing his teeth (or lack of them).

Yes, the gaffer provoked a furious dust-up in Bradford's penalty area early on with a challenge on their goalkeeper. I think the ball was 60-40 in the keeper's favour as they went for it and Joe put his foot in as he tended to do as the tough player he was. There was a tremendous fracas with players from both teams involved and when it calmed down he was booked. These days the card might have been a different colour! It went on to be a brilliant night for us. The crowd was more than 15,000, but our 3,000 supporters shouted themselves hoarse and that inspired us to cling on.

The semi-final draw paired you with probably the best team in the country at the time in Brian Clough's Nottingham Forest, with the first leg away at the City Ground. What are your recollections of that evening?

Alan in the home dressing room at Ashton Gate with then player-manager Joe Jordan

The first memory is of the trip from our hotel to the ground because it proved a nightmare. We seemed to have left in plenty of time, but the coach driver, Stuart, who was known to take a wrong turning occasionally, couldn't find a way off the main road. We could see the stadium in the distance but kept going back and forth across a bridge over the River Trent without getting any nearer. Time was going on and we ended up getting changed on the coach. By the time we got to the ground we had on our full strip, with only our boots left to put on. It was into the dressing room to hang our stuff on a peg, on with the boots and straight out onto the pitch

Alan in League Cup semi-final action being challenged by Nottingham Forest's Neil Webb

with the game about to start.

In those days warm-ups only lasted about ten minutes, but we hardly had time even for that. I think in a way it helped because there were no moments to dwell on what lay ahead and suffer any nerves. Forest were a brilliant team and Keith Waugh had another fantastic game, while we defended well as a team in front of him. Then with about 25 minutes to go we took the lead. I crossed a ball that eluded a few players, Joe challenged for it and Mark Gavin laid it into the path of Paul Mardon, whose shot flew into the corner of the net. We were almost as shocked as Forest and the first thought was "can we hang on?" It so nearly happened, but five minutes from the end John Pender stuck out a leg, trying to divert a ball into our box out for a corner, and it agonisingly rolled past 'Woffy' into the net for an own goal.

The 1-1 draw, celebrated by 8,000 travelling City fans, drew amazement throughout the country. It was a fantastic achievement for a Third Division team.

Forest's team was full of internationals, so it was a proud night for us. They were going well in the old First Division and had put a few teams to the sword in the League Cup, beating Chester 10-0 on aggregate in the second round. A lot of people expected us to suffer a similar fate. The other semi-final between Luton Town and West Ham was thought likely to be a lot closer and ours such a foregone conclusion that it was not decided to screen the second leg at Ashton Gate live on TV until after the first leg had been played in case Forest were out of sight. As it turned out Luton beat West Ham comfortably and our tie provided all the drama.

A crowd of more than 28,000 packed Ashton Gate for the second leg and a television audience of millions saw City come within inches of reaching a major Wembley final. You, above all, have good reason to remember the game.

It was a dreadful day of cold wet weather, with strong wind and the rain lashing down. The pitch was heavy and proved a bit of a leveller, so we had good reason to think a shock was on. Joe Jordan got things tactically spot-on over the two legs. We had gone to the City Ground to defend and maybe nick a goal, which is what happened, and at home we played the same way. Forest had the majority of the play again, but didn't manage to break us

down until extra time, largely because of Keith Waugh saves and all of us defending for our lives. With just a little luck in the final minute of normal time, we would have won and gone to Wembley.

You are talking about your shot that hit a post at a time when Forest would have had little chance of responding. Talk us through that moment.

Steve McClaren took a corner and John Pender flicked the ball on. It fell behind me just around the penalty spot and I was facing our goal as I turned and hit it. There were a lot of players between me and the Forest net, but I had a good sight of the shot, which I think went between someone's legs before coming back off the post. Their keeper couldn't see where it had gone and Rob Newman moved in on the rebound, looking certain to score. Unfortunately, one of the Forest players just got there before him and put it out for another corner. That one was delivered straight into the keeper's hands, he threw it out to Franz Carr, who raced up the pitch with us all chasing him, desperate to get back.

He put in a cross, which I think Neil Webb headed into Keith Waugh's arms and the ref blew the whistle to signal extra time. Even then, we were only five minutes or so away from earning a replay at Villa Park when Garry Parker struck the winning goal. It was desperately disappointing, but another game against such great opponents would have been tough as that season we had already played six FA Cup games, four of them in a second round tie against Aldershot, which went to three replays, in a campaign that involved 64 matches overall.

Any memories of the inimitable Brian Clough from those epic battles?

Not so much from those two games because he was serving a touchline ban for clouting a couple of fans, who were part of a pitch invasion in an earlier round. But when I was at Darlington the club were going through financial problems and played Forest in a benefit game at our small ground to raise some funds. After the match I was walking down a corridor, drinking from a bottle of beer I had in my hand when I saw Brian walking towards me. "Were you the number ten?" he asked and I told him "Yes", to which he responded "If you could cross and play those cross-field passes like that every week you would be playing in the First Division."

Boldly, I told him: "I can do it every week" and he said: "In that case I have a bit of advice for you young man." By this time I was getting a bit excited so I asked what it was. "Don't drink out of bottles," says Cloughie and walks off!

A big move never materialised, despite your many great goals and countless assists for City and you ended up being transferred to Turkish club Besiktas. How would you sum up your five years at Ashton Gate?

They were some of the best and happiest days of my career. I was lucky to join City at a time when everyone knitted together and we had a wonderful squad of players. A lot of that was due to Terry Cooper and his assistant Clive Middlemass, who had rebuilt the club from almost going out of business in 1982 and fostered a great spirit in not just the team, but among the staff

Joe Jordan and Jimmy Lumsden built on that when they took charge. We never won promotion during my time, which was disappointing because we had the quality of players to do it, but two Wembley finals in the Freight Rover Trophy, including the win over Bolton in 1986, were highlights, as was the League Cup run. The fans were brilliant to me and there were so many games that stand out. Wonderful times.

CLIVE WHITEHEAD

1972-1981

Clive Whitehead joined City as a teenager and became part of the squad Alan Dicks fashioned, which took the club into the top flight of English football. The exciting winger netted the winner against Portsmouth at Ashton Gate on April 20th 1976, which clinched a place in the old First Division, and went on to pose problems for the best full-backs in the country during the following seasons.

You come from the Midlands so how was it that you signed for City?

I was with Wolves as a kid and then I started playing local football in Birmingham for a team called Northfield Juniors. We drew Bristol City in the FA Youth Cup in the autumn of 1972 and after that game I was offered a trial at Ashton Gate, which proved successful and led to the club signing me. I remember being very excited to be in Bristol with the opportunity to launch a professional career.

What do you remember of the early years?

I would say the work that went into the promotion success of 1976 probably began 18 months or more before it happened, with Alan Dicks building the side. When I first arrived, the club were around mid-table in the Second Division attracting crowds of between 10,000 and 12,000. Turning those figures into the 38,000, who watched us play at home in the First Division took a lot of effort from everyone involved and it certainly didn't happen overnight. By the time I got into the side on a regular basis in the middle of the 1975-76 season, replacing Mike Brolly, the team were up and running with all the key components in place.

So let's move on to the promotion season. What made that side so effective and at what stage did you start to think you could achieve something special?

There were fantastic players in all positions. We had two great strikers in Paul Cheesley and Tom Ritchie and my job was straightforward, to create a bit of space on either flank and supply them with decent crosses. I knew if I did that often enough one of them would

Whitehead scores winner after three minutes

Bristol City 1, Portsmouth 0

BRISTOL CITY are back in the First Division after a break of 65 years, but they were made to fight all the way before clinching promotion with a 1-0 win over bottom-of-the-table Portsmouth at Ashton Gate last night.

It was an historical night and Bristol's biggest soccer occasion in 70 years since the City club reached the First Division for the first time in 1907.

City had the incentive of a third-minute goal, but the tension lasted all through the match.

Thousands of fans invaded the pitch after the game, and when the players finally reached their dressing room to be welcomed

HERBERT GILLAM

at Ashton Gate

Gillies, and Ritchie, who cut inside and pulled the ball

A sliced lob across his own goal by Merrick had the crowd gasping, it was an incredible risk and one which would have spelt trouble had a Portsmouth player been on hand.

It restored a sense of urgency in City's play, however, and Cheesley came desperately close to a goal when he hammered the ball against the top of the Portsmouth bar from 20 yards out, with goalkeeper Figgins well beaten.

As a striking force there was really only one team in it, Tainton also being robbed of a goal by Figgins.

Clive Whitehead, right, fires in the goal which brought Bristol City promotion to the First Division. Below, Whitehead shows his jubilation with a victory leap.

be in the right position to score. It was a wonderful season in so many respects because we gelled together so well on and off the pitch. One of my first games coming into the side was away at Oldham Athletic, who were a good team and tough to beat on their own ground. We won 4-2 and absolutely slaughtered them, so we had a hunch something was happening.

Later we beat York City 4-1 at Ashton Gate and the game featured on Match of the Day. Tom Ritchie netted a hat-trick and by then we were all convinced that we had what it took to sustain a promotion challenge. Between then and the final couple of games we were really flying and got some great results. People remember the Scottish contingent in the squad, but what made it more unusual was the number of Bristol lads. I doubt there has been as many in a City squad since. Only Ipswich Town at the time probably matched us for home grown talent.

The climax came against a young Portsmouth side in front of a 27,000 Ashton Gate crowd, buzzing with expectation. What do you recall of that night and your winning goal?

All I remember about the goal is that Brian Drysdale had the ball out on the left and fed a cross in for Paul Cheesley, who just got a little flick on it. Of course, being the player I was, I read where the ball would go and volleyed it in. What a strike! I can tell you now that if the ball hadn't hit the back of the net it would have ended up in Long Ashton. The next thing I knew all the other players were jumping on me. But there was a problem. It was only the third or fourth minute and for the rest of the match we were so on edge about what we might achieve that we didn't play well. It seemed to me that we spent the remaining 87 minutes defending. Everyone was thinking that we just had to get the match over and be promoted. Tension grew in the crowd, with supporters virtually encroaching onto the pitch, and although it all sounds fantastic now, it was a horrible game by the standards we had set. Portsmouth, who were at the bottom of the table, were actually the better team on the night. Pressure does strange things to you. For the whole of that season we had been bossing some very good sides, including the likes of Sunderland and West Bromwich Albion, who we visited in the space of a week and came away with a draw and a victory. We dealt with those challenges brilliantly, but when it came to getting across the finishing line it proved very tough. Having won promotion, we lost our last game at home to Notts County the following Saturday, although – and this is just for you Richard because you always dig me out about not getting enough goals – I scored in that match as well. It was a tap-in and that's all I can remember about it. We had been celebrating for three days. The 1970s were a time when footballers socialised a lot and we used to go out regularly as a group because we all got on so well. So we did have a few drinks that week. I remember Notts County's players forming a guard of honour when we ran out onto the pitch, but the game itself is a total blur.

Division One here we come – Clive leaps to celebrate his goal against Portsmouth that took City back to the top flight after an absence of 65 years

Moving forward a few months, the eagerly-awaited First Division campaign began at one of the country's most famous stadiums, Highbury, against the might of Arsenal. It proved another memorable day.
We had been playing some decent sides in the Second Division, but suddenly we find ourselves visiting one of the biggest clubs in the country. Arsenal had just paid a record fee of more than £300,000 to sign Malcolm MacDonald and had a World Cup winner in Alan Ball playing for them. People were saying we might get beaten by five or six goals, but we never felt that way and as individuals we were all looking forward to the match.

Arriving at Highbury, we found it a bit strange, but once we got out onto the pitch we took a look around and thought "we can play here". Later we found that you did get a bit more time on the ball in the First Division, but then it was all new to us. We knew we had good players and as the game developed we were sure we could win. Paul Cheesley battered the Arsenal centre-backs David O'Leary and Peter Simpson in the air and he and Tom Ritchie really made a mark that day. The only surprise was that we only scored once. With the chances we had, we could easily have won by four or five. I can only recall Ray Cashley having to deal with one long-range shot from Arsenal and no one

Clive returns to the scene of his historic goal 24 hours after netting the winner against Portsmouth

could argue that our victory wasn't fully deserved.

Three days later Stoke City came to Ashton Gate and an incident that appeared none too serious at the time had a devastating effect on the team's future.

Paul Cheesley damaged a cruciate ligament and other areas of a knee in a challenge with goalkeeper Peter Shilton, having shown just how good a player he was becoming when netting the winner at Arsenal. He was the catalyst for taking us as far as we had come. Back then not a great deal was known about cruciate injuries and we thought Paul would be back after a few games. He did eventually return for a home match against Birmingham City, but it was obvious he wasn't the same. Paul had everything. He was a good finisher, great upstairs and quick, as well as aggressive. Tom Ritchie played off of him well and worked his socks off, so it was a really effective combination. Sometimes they had a go at me for beating a defender twice while they were waiting for a cross, but I used to get enjoyment out of that. The biggest compliment I can pay 'Cheese' is that he was like an Alan Shearer, only with more height. I played with the likes of Paul Mariner and Cyrille Regis, who were great strikers, but 'Cheese' had more potential. None of us know how good a side we could have become if he had stayed fit or how long I would have continued to play on the wing, with him and Tom to feed. But I truly believe we would have done well. The only thing is that had Paul carried on playing he wouldn't have stayed at Bristol City for long.

You took the First Division by storm, with top full-backs regularly picking up bookings trying to mark you, but as your City career developed you became a defender yourself. How did that happen?

With Tom and 'Cheese' up front, the three of us had caused teams a lot of problems. I saw plenty of the ball, which I enjoyed. We then signed Joe Royle to replace Paul and, while he had been a hell of a player and was a really great bloke, he was approaching the end of his career. He didn't have the same impact and I started to feel a bit isolated playing on the wing. I wasn't enjoying my football as much and when you don't see a lot of the ball, there is more pressure to do something when you get it. I had always fancied playing

YOU CAN'T CHOP THIS KID DOWN

By GRAHAM RUSSELL

BRISTOL CITY have told Don Revie that get-up-and-go winger Clive Whitehead is ready for his England Under-21 squad.

Whitehead has burst into the First Division with eye-catching games . . . yet last winter he took to selling petrol on the forecourt when Wolves turned him down.

He wondered if he had a future. And so did City. They recognised his talent but there were question marks against his guts and his stamina.

After one poor match his manager, Alan Dicks, vowed he was going to keep him in the reserves for three months. Inside two he had to change his mind.

Now with No. 11 on his back but operating down the right, Whitehead is rapidly becoming a marked player . . . and enjoying every minute.

City No. 2 Tony Collins says: "Just look at the way he's turning backs of international standard.

"Look at what he did to Nelson at Arsenal. The fella was backing off, twisting and wondering what to do next.

Finally he chopped him down and was booked. But Whitehead still got the cross which brought us the win.

"At Newcastle he had Kennedy, an Under-23 cap, going all ways. Pejic, Stoke's international, stopped him by being booked. And when Coventry came here in the week they put two men on him."

Success against the top players hasn't surprised Whitehead, who drew a £70,000 bid from Spurs after his first game for City when he inspired them to a 2—0 win at Millwall.

He had the top backs summed up as a spectator.

"There are big differences in skills between the first two divisions but as I watched the First Division games from the terraces I kept noticing how much space they seemed to give." he says.

"In these first few games I found it to be true. The freedom they give you is surprising."

No one at Ashton Gate expects 90 minutes lung-bursting effort from him. But what about that faint heart?

Whitehead smiles. "It's all a question of being involved. The team are so great I'm in there all the time and they see me up and keep me going."

His manager, Dicks, explores that explanation. Whitehead's problems, he thinks, were all in the head. Although he has the skill mentally he couldn't go forward.

"Now, in the First Division, he's prepared to go inside and he doesn't turn if in when he's whacked." said Dicks. "I was told once he's chicken. But he's not.

"Defences are worried because he can turn them and work either flank. He knows now he has to be kicked and come back without flinching because referees aren't going to protect him."

"For a lad who won't be 21 until November and has only 40-odd games behind him, Whitehead has quite a reputation. Are you reading me Mr. Revie?

further back and thought that coming from deeper areas to go past opponents would suit me. I tried it and for the next ten years I plied my trade at right-back, left-back or in the centre of defence. When City had their financial troubles at the start of the 1980s I moved to West Bromwich Albion, where I became captain, and loved every minute of playing for another fabulous club.

But the times at Ashton Gate were unforgettable. We all got on so well, built something together and bought into the way the manager wanted to play, It was an amazing time to be in Bristol because the city went with us and I like to think we changed it with our success. To see 38,000 fans fill the ground was quite something and I only hope it happens again one day. What we proved was that the people are out there to back top flight football and they just need a team to provide it.

BRISTOL'S SUBS BENCH

ERRATA

Dates should read:

Page 52: Rob Edwards – 1991-1999

Page 73: Chris Honor – 1985-1991

Page 119: Gary Owers – 1994-1998

Page 131: Tom Ritchie – 1972-1981 & 1982-1984

Page 169: Brian Tinnion – 1993-2005